Pixie Turner (Plantbased Pixie) is a a food blogger, biochemist (BSc),
nutritionist (MSc) (AfN), writer, and speaker. She has also been
featured at many events, in various publications and on
BBC World News and Channel 5 as a nutritional expert.

WWW.PIXIETURNERNUTRITION.COM

Pixie's
PLATES

70 PLANT-RICH RECIPES FROM
PIXIE TURNER

HEAD of ZEUS

An Anima Book

ISBN (PB): 9781789541076
ISBN (E): 9781789541083

Design and lettering by Natalie Samuelson
Printed and bound in Spain by Graficas Estella

Head of Zeus Ltd
5–8 Hardwick Street
London EC1R 4RG
www.headofzeus.com

CONTENTS

Introduction

Let's kick things off on the right foot to avoid any awkward confusion later on: this isn't a diet book, and it's not a clean-eating bible, transformation plan or miracle cure. It's about celebrating food in all its glory, because food is something wonderful and delicious and incredible, and all too often it's a source of fear and anxiety for people.

We live in a world of misinformation, with sensationalist headlines and misleading influencer posts on Instagram on a daily basis. It's no wonder really that pseudoscience and nutrition myths have been allowed to thrive. We like simple solutions, and we're much more comfortable with black and white, good and bad foods; eat this but don't eat that. It's the reason that we, as a general rule, don't follow government guidelines very well. The five-a-day message has been out there for ages now, and yet as a population we aren't meeting that. Telling us to eat more of something is far less effective than telling us to cut foods out, and that's where wellness thrives.

Food packaging will proudly display everything it's 'free from' (soy, gluten, sugar, eggs, joy. . .) because what you don't eat is now more of a status symbol than what you do. If you look at any famous wellness blogger (or at least their 'food philosophy'), you'll find a list of foods that are deemed unacceptable, whether it's all animal products, gluten, legumes or grains. There's always something. Most commonly of all: processed foods, gluten and refined sugar. Hopefully, by the end of this book, you'll agree with me that it's just bollocks.

All of us fall for misinformation sometimes, but that's ok. It's okay to make mistakes, to admit to being in the wrong, to change and improve based on evidence. That's good scientific practice and I think we all need to be a little more sceptical and a little more scientific. I freely admit I made mistakes: I fell for pretty much every nugget of pseudoscience handed to me by wellness bloggers, including (but not limited to) cutting out endless food groups from my diet, believing I needed 'superfood' powders to be healthy, thinking refined sugar is toxic, not eating gluten, juicing for health, feeling the need to 'detox' my body and even doing week-long raw vegan 'cleanses'. I attached a moral compass to food. I'm not perfect, but I've learnt from these mistakes; I've taken on board new evidence and improved my understanding of nutrition and health. I've definitely made some enemies of those who were not fans of me calling them out on their fearmongering, but I believe if you haven't pissed off a few people along the way and caused a little controversy, then you haven't really achieved something new and exciting. To me, it's a sign I'm doing something right. I'm now going to help you do the same using the tools at my disposal – scientific evidence, beautiful and delicious food and a dash of sarcasm.

Each chapter in this book is going to give you a brief overview of a common nutritional myth that has plagued both the wellness industry and mainstream media – everything from gluten and raw food to detoxing and superfoods. I'm going to tackle each one with the real science behind the myth, separating fact from fiction, and show you how to put this information into practice in the form of delicious, no-BS, fad-free recipes.

In reality, the basics of good nutrition are extremely simple: eat a varied, balanced diet, with a little bit of what you fancy. Basically, everything in moderation. It sounds boring and that's why it's not popular – it doesn't sell books, doesn't get TV ratings and doesn't inspire miracle cures or miracle foods. There is no quick or easy solution; it's not down to individual foods or nutrients, it's down to eating a variety of foods in the long term and not over-indulging in anything – even kale!

Ultimately, a healthy diet should not come at the expense of a healthy relationship with food –there's little point eating the healthiest diet in the world only to end up a one-hundred-year-old miserable person. Because good health comes down to more than just eating well; it's having an overall healthy lifestyle including regular exercise, a good sleep pattern, the ability to cope with stress, genetics, good mental health, happiness and a balanced diet. Lack of sleep and high stress levels are often underplayed, when they can have a huge effect on wellbeing. Mental health is overlooked most of all, and socioeconomic factors barely even get a mention.

We too quickly forget that the populations who live the longest thrive on vastly varying diets, eat slowly and mindfully, and eat socially. They are proof that there is no one-size-fits-all solution to happiness and longevity. And this is why I will not tell you that there is one single way to eat, one single way to be healthy and won't give you a list of food rules to follow or foods to avoid. What I can give you is permission to eat foods that make you happy, and to not give a shit about what others think. Eat that cake, but also eat those vegetables, too.

The focus here is on celebrating foods that have had a bit of a rough time in terms of PR lately – foods like bread, cheese, eggs, and cakes made with caster sugar. I'm a firm believer that health is about more than just the nutrients found in food, and that when we celebrate and enjoy food, not see it as something to be feared, it enriches our lives and means we're far less likely to overeat and feel guilt and shame.

Are you ready? Let's dive in . . .

Gluten

THE GLUTEN MYTH

Gluten is a group of proteins, composed of mainly gliadin and glutenin.
If you suffer from coeliac disease your body produces an autoimmune reaction to
the gliadin part of the gluten protein (in most cases, at least). For the vast majority
of the population who don't have coeliac disease, the body simply digests gluten just
like any other protein. Gluten is found in grains like wheat, spelt, barley and rye.
It gives elasticity to dough, helps it keep its shape and gives a chewy texture.
The name comes from its glue-like properties.

Coeliac disease is a serious condition, for which exclusion of gluten is
the only solution. But most people who are eliminating gluten from their diets
have no medical basis for doing so. Non-coeliac gluten sensitivity (NCGS)
is still being debated as to how real it is, and while it does seem like a small
group of people to suffer with this, it's still not recommended for everyone
to simply cut out gluten in case.

A key to gut health, and therefore overall health, is having a varied diet with
a whole range of foods. So why not let that include grains and gluten? (Unless
you have coeliac disease.) It'll make your social life easier, it'll make you happier
and it'll mean you can try all the delicious gluten-containing and gluten-free
recipes in this chapter. I've based my decision of grain purely on taste,
texture and ease, not on whether it contains gluten or not.

Everything is chemicals. Everything you eat and breathe is made of chemicals

The gluten-free trend is a classic example of the elitism of the wellness industry - if it's more expensive, it's more desirable, because it discriminates and shows that you can afford to spend money on something more expensive, even though you don't really need to

BLACK RICE WITH BUTTERNUT SQUASH AND CHARD

SERVES 4-6

- 250g black rice
- 1 tbsp soy sauce
- ½ lemon, juiced
- 400g butternut squash, peeled and cubed
- Olive oil
- Salt and pepper
- 150g rainbow chard, roughly chopped
- 1 red pepper, cubed
- Fresh coriander leaves, to serve

Black rice, like all rice, is naturally gluten-free and delicious. Black rice has the mildest effect on blood sugar levels, so if you love your grains but find they don't always work for you, this might be the one to try. Me? I just love the colour!

Preheat the oven to 200°C fan/220°C conventional/gas mark 7.

Cook the rice in boiling water with the soy sauce and lemon juice according to the packet instructions, but for 1 minute less than stated.

Spread the butternut squash over a baking tray, drizzle with olive oil and season with salt and pepper. Roast in the oven for around 30 minutes, until soft.

When the rice is cooked, remove from the heat, drain any remaining water and stir in the chard. Leave the lid on for another 5 minutes.

Add the butternut squash and red pepper to the rice, stir and season to taste.

Serve in a big bowl with fresh coriander on top.

TIP If you're a meat-eater, this recipe would also taste great with chicken.

BREAKFAST IN BREAD

SERVES 1 HUNGRY PERSON

- 1 small sourdough loaf
- 20g spinach leaves
- 80g tomatoes, sliced
- 50g white or chestnut mushrooms, sliced
- 1 medium egg, separated
- Salt and pepper
- 50g grated cheddar cheese

I love a good food pun. I saw something like this in a viral video on social media around the time I was recipe testing and knew straight away this was something I needed to make. I just love bread. To avoid wasting any bread, you can turn the scooped out insides into croutons!

Preheat the oven to 180°C fan/200°C conventional/gas mark 6. Cut the top off the loaf and hollow it out.

Lay the spinach leaves in the bottom, followed by slices of tomato and mushroom.

Mix the egg white with a little salt and pepper and pour into the cracks. Cover with the grated cheese and bake in the oven for 30 minutes.

Gently place the egg yolk on top and bake for another 2 minutes.

Cut into quarters to serve.

COUSCOUS SALAD

SERVES 6-8

- 200g couscous
- ½ vegetable stock cube
- ½ lemon, zested and juiced
- 2 tbsp olive oil
- 200g feta, cubed
- 150g cucumber, cubed
- 1 orange or yellow pepper, cubed
- 150g tomatoes, diced
- 1 x 400g tin of chickpeas, drained and rinsed
- 100g pomegranate seeds
- Large handful of fresh herbs (as many of the following as possible: basil, flat-leaf parsley, chives, oregano, mint, thyme, sage), finely sliced
- Salt and pepper
- Halved lemons, to serve

You don't see many wellness bloggers eating couscous . . . Maybe because it's not gluten-free? Couscous is made from wheat, so lots of gluten there. But it's one of the easiest and quickest grains to cook – just add hot water. Literally.

Measure out the couscous into a large bowl.

Mix 300ml of boiling water with the vegetable stock cube, the lemon zest and juice and the olive oil. Pour over the couscous and leave for 10 minutes.

Fluff up the couscous with a fork.

Add the feta, cucumber, pepper, tomatoes, chickpeas, pomegranate seeds and herbs to the couscous and season with salt and pepper. Stir to combine and serve with halved lemons.

 TIP Add a little hot stock to leftovers the next day to freshen them up.

HAZELNUT & CRANBERRY GRANOLA

SERVES 4-6

- 150g rolled oats (other kinds work well too)
- 30g ground flaxseed
- 50g chopped hazelnuts
- 50g whole hazelnuts
- 3 tbsp olive oil
- 4 tbsp maple syrup or rice syrup (maple is sweeter)
- 100g dried cranberries
- Yoghurt and fresh fruit, to serve

Oats are one of the few grains that pretty much everyone in wellness, from fitness bloggers to fake nutritionists, can agree are good for you. We've had overnight oats, zoats (porridge with shredded courgette) and proats (porridge with added protein). We've had an avalanche of porridge recipes, so I don't feel a particularly strong urge to contribute to that – pretty much anyone can make porridge. So here's some granola instead.

Preheat the oven to 150°C fan/170°C conventional/gas mark 3. Mix together the oats, flaxseed and chopped and whole hazelnuts.

Add the olive oil and syrup and mix into the dry ingredients until thoroughly combined.

Spread the mixture out quite thinly over a baking tray and bake in the oven for 15 minutes. The mixture should be crunchy by this point. If not, bake for another 5–10 minutes.

Add the cranberries and stir gently. Bake for another 5 minutes.

Allow to cool slightly before handling the mixture so that the clusters hold their shape.

Store in an airtight container and serve with yoghurt and fresh fruit for breakfast.

TRICOLORE PESTO PENNE

SERVES 4

- 250g penne (around 600g cooked)
- 95g basil pesto
- 150g plum tomatoes, halved
- 1 large avocado, cubed
- 150g mini mozzarella balls
- 1 tbsp fresh basil leaves, shredded

Pasta is an ideal, quick, no-fuss lunch or dinner option and this recipe is particularly speedy. I'm not even expecting you to make your own pesto, although you can if you want to, of course. Use regular, whole wheat or gluten-free pasta, I won't judge. Just make sure to cook it for 1 minute less than packet instructions to get perfectly al dente pasta that isn't overcooked!

Bring a large saucepan of salted water to the boil.

Add the penne and cook for 10 minutes (or 1 minute less than the packet states).

When cooked, drain the water from the penne and coat in pesto.

Add the tomatoes, avocado cubes, mozzarella balls and shredded basil leaves and mix together.

Serve immediately.

TIP This recipe tastes great cold too! Simply refresh leftovers with a little extra pesto or olive oil.

SANDWICHES THREE WAYS

Cheesy sandwich
- ½ medium avocado, mashed
- Salt and pepper
- 3 slices of mature cheddar cheese
- ¼ red pepper
- Small handful of salad leaves

Yoghurty aubergine sandwich
- ½ small aubergine, sliced into rings
- Olive oil
- Salt and pepper
- 80g yoghurt
- 1 tsp chives
- 4-6 slices of cucumber

Sprinkling of cress

Smoked Tofu and Hummus Sandwich
- 40g hummus
- 50g firm smoked tofu, sliced
- 1 small carrot, grated
- Small handful of spinach leaves

In wellness, avocado toast is acceptable, but top with another slice of bread and it becomes something evil: a sandwich! Sandwiches are far too mainstream for wellness, but there's nothing to be afraid of. A sandwich can be a wonderful, nutritious meal. Here are three delocious examples of fillings to put between two slices of bread.

Cheesy sandwich

Season the avocado and spread three-quarters on one slice of bread and the rest on a second slice. Place the cheese slices on top of the thicker avocado, followed by the pepper and salad leaves, then put the second piece of bread on top.

Yoghurty aubergine sandwich

Drizzle the aubergine with olive oil and season. Heat a griddle pan until hot and grill the aubergine slices on both sides until cooked. Mix together the yoghurt and chives and season with salt and pepper Spread the yoghurt on two slices of bread. Place the aubergine on one of the pieces of bread, followed by the sliced cucumber and a sprinkling of cress, then put the second piece of bread on top.

Smoked tofu & hummus sandwich

Spread the hummus on two slices of bread. Place the tofu on one of the slices, followed by the carrot and spinach, then top with the second piece of bread.

PIXIE'S BEGINNERS SOURDOUGH

MAKES 1 LOAF

For the leaven
- 20g starter
- 220g strong white flour

For the loaf
- 350g leaven
- 100g wholemeal bread flour
- 220g strong white flour
- 9g salt

You will need:
- A scraper
- A proving basket or large bowl
- A Dutch oven or two baking trays
- A lot of patience - this recipe takes 2 days to make!

I LOVE BREAD and I find making it very therapeutic. I learnt to make sourdough at the E5 Bakehouse in London, and that's where I get my starter every time I kill one (which happens more often than I care to admit). If you're a newbie to sourdough, start with a recipe like this, which focuses on white flour as it's much easier to bake with.

To make the leaven, mix together the starter and 170ml of lukewarm water, then add the flour and mix with your hands to combine. It should look like image 1. Cover the bowl with a tea towel and set aside for 8-24 hours, depending on the conditions; 8 hours if it's a warm sunny day or closer to 24 hours if it's a cold winter's day. You want it to be stringy and full of holes when you break the surface.

To make the loaf, weigh out 350g of the leaven you made the day before and add 210ml of water. Use your fingers to rub the mixture to combine it with the water until there are no lumps (see image 2). Don't use a rigorous stirring method; be gentle with it.

Add the wholemeal and white flours and combine into a single mass. Don't worry if it's still very sticky at this point (see image 3). Leave for 20 minutes.

Place the mixture on a floured surface, form a well and add the salt. Fold the edges of the dough over so the salt is inside and work the dough to disperse the salt. Place back in the bowl and leave for 30 minutes. It should now be a ball like in image 4. >

PIXIE'S BEGINNERS SOURDOUGH cont.

Stretch and fold a section of the dough (see images 5 and 6) without letting the dough break. This forms a rough triangle with the piece you've folded (the top of the triangle is in the centre of the dough and the two corners the edges); take hold of one of those corners and repeat the stretch and fold. Repeat this once all the way around. Flip the dough over and place your hands on either side of the dough. Move both hands in a clockwise motion, while tucking the dough slightly under, to form a ball shape (without it losing contact with the work surface). Place it back into the bowl and leave for 30 minutes.

Repeat the stretch and fold, leave for 30 minutes. Repeat the stretch and fold again, leave for 30 minutes. Form the dough into a ball and sprinkle generously with flour. Place it seam-side up in a proving basket (or a bowl with enough space for it to grow) (see image 7) and leave to prove for 60–90 minutes.

Preheat the oven to its highest temperature. Put a Dutch oven or lined baking tray in the oven to warm, then fill another baking tray with boiling water and place this in the bottom of the oven.

Carefully place the loaf in the hot Dutch oven or on the hot baking tray and bake for 30 minutes with the lid on the Dutch oven or with the tray of water, then for another 10 minutes without the lid or tray.

The loaf is ready when nicely browned on top (see image 8) and when the base sounds hollow when tapped. Leave to cool before slicing (see image 9).

SPELT WITH HALLOUMI & SWEET POTATO

SERVES 2

- 200g sweet potatoes
- Olive oil
- Salt and pepper
- 150g pearled spelt
- 1 tbsp tahini
- 60g spinach leaves, roughly chopped
- 150g tomatoes, roughly chopped
- 1 tbsp fresh mint leaves, roughly chopped
- 100g halloumi

Spelt is a more unusual grain. Yes, it contains gluten, which is probably at least partly why it hasn't reached the same popularity level as quinoa. If you can't find spelt, rice would work very well instead.

Preheat the oven to 200°C fan/220°C conventional/gas mark 7.

Peel and chop the sweet potatoes into cubes and place on a lined baking tray. Drizzle with olive oil, season with salt and pepper and roast in the oven for 20-30 minutes, until soft.

Cook the spelt in a saucepan of boiling salted water for 20 minutes.

Drain any excess water and stir in the tahini, along with a little salt to taste.

Add the chopped spinach to the spelt. Replace the lid to let it wilt slightly.

Add the cooked sweet potato, tomatoes and chopped mint to the pan and mix everything together. Transfer to a serving dish or two plates.

Fry the halloumi in a dry frying pan and place on top of the salad. Serve immediately before the cheese becomes rubbery.

TIP If you are making this in advance, don't fry the halloumi until you're ready to eat.

TOMATO & COURGETTE RISOTTO

SERVES 4-6

- Olive oil
- 1 onion (around 110g), peeled and diced
- 1 vegetable stock cube
- 400g risotto rice
- 1 x 400g tin of chopped tomatoes
- 1 courgette (around 250g), coarsely grated
- 100g cherry tomatoes, halved
- 2 garlic cloves, peeled
- Large handful of fresh basil leaves
- Coarse sea salt
- 25g butter or vegan margarine
- 100g finely grated Parmesan, plus extra for sprinkling (leave out to make it vegan)

Most vegetarians will have had at least one bad risotto experience in their life. Mushroom risotto is the typical veggie option on a meat-focused menu, and it often feels like a cop-out. A risotto like this one was made for me at an event with chef Theo Randall, and it was the first time I tasted risotto and loved it. It was perfection. So, naturally, I went home and tried my best to recreate it from the vague instructions I remembered. I'd say it's just as good as his, but don't tell him that. Oh, and it's gluten-free!

Heat 2 tablespoons of olive oil in a wide, straight-sided frying pan over a medium heat. Cook the onion for around 5 minutes, making sure it doesn't burn.

In the meantime, cover the vegetable stock cube with 500ml of boiling water and stir until dissolved.

Add the rice to the frying pan and heat through, stirring continuously for a few minutes.

Add half the stock, stir thoroughly, then add the chopped tomatoes. Cook the rice for 15 minutes or 2 minutes less than recommended by the packet instructions, stirring continuously.

Cook the courgette separately in a little olive oil to remove any excess moisture. >

TOMATO & COURGETTE RISOTTO cont.

It's a bit of a juggling act, but stir both pans continuously to avoid the rice sticking to the bottom of the pan (turn down the heat if necessary) and to avoid burning the courgette. If the rice gets too dry, add a some of the remaining stock, a little at a time. If it bubbles too much, turn down the heat a little.

Once the courgette has lost most of its moisture, stir it into the rice. Add a little more oil to the pan that the courgettes were in and gently cook the cherry tomatoes until soft.

In a pestle and mortar, crush the garlic and basil to a paste with a little sea salt and add to the risotto. If you don't have a pestle and mortar, then use a small food processor or finely chopping by hand would work too.

When the rice has been cooking for 15 minutes, taste the risotto. It should be al dente, not completely soft. If it's ready, turn off the heat and stir in the cherry tomatoes. Stir through the butter and half the Parmesan, if using.

Serve immediately, adding a sprinkling of Parmesan and a final drizzle of olive oil (trust me on this one, don't skip it) to each individual plate.

VANILLA WAFFLES WITH STRAWBERRY COMPOTE

MAKES 1 WAFFLE

- 100g chopped strawberries (fresh or frozen)
- 1 tbsp maple syrup
- 50g plain or wholemeal flour
- 1 tsp baking powder
- Pinch of salt
- 1 tsp vanilla bean paste or essence
- 1 tbsp sugar or 1 tsp stevia
- 1 egg, beaten
- 50ml milk (cows, oat or almond)
- Greek yoghurt (optional)

I used to make vegan and gluten-free pancakes, and now I look back and have no idea how I managed that. Pancakes and waffles taste so much better with gluten in them. If you don't have a waffle iron, you can easily make these into pancakes instead!

Put the strawberries and maple syrup into a small saucepan, along with a splash of water if using fresh berries. Cook gently until it becomes thick and jam-like. This will take anywhere between 5–20 minutes depending on the berries.

Mix together the rest of the ingredients (minus the yoghurt) and stir until thoroughly combined.

Pour into a preheated waffle iron and cook for around 5 minutes, until golden brown.

When ready, serve with the strawberry compote and yoghurt (if using).

Detox

THE DETOXING MYTH

Whether it's green juice, detox teas, coffee enemas, or IV vitamin drips, these 'detox' methods all claim to be able to rid your body of toxins in some way. But what's missing from all of the 'detox' methods out there is a mechanism. They can't even name the toxins they're supposedly getting rid of!

You just need a liver and kidneys to detox, they do all the work, performing complex reactions to convert toxic substances into ones that are safe for excretion. In general, people might feel better after a 'detox' simply because they're drinking less alcohol and getting more nutrients, that's all! On the flip side, any negative symptoms that are often associated with things like juice cleanses are always twisted into simply being signs that the detox is working. Whilst this is a clever marketing tactic, it's also absolutely rubbish. If you're feeling dizzy and nauseous, you're not 'detoxing', you're probably just really hungry and need food.

Detoxification is a scientific principle that's been hijacked by the wellness industry, and is wrapped in a scientific banner in an attempt to give the treatments and practitioners credibility. Having said all that, eating a balanced diet and not drinking too much alcohol is still a good idea! More specifically, it seems that there are some foods like broccoli which may have more of an effect on your liver than other foods due to their chemical make-up. The following recipes all contain foods like these, and no green juice in sight!

Detoxification is a scientific principle that's been hijacked by the wellness industry, and is wrapped in a scientific banner in an attempt to give the treatments and practitioners credibility

ALOO DUM

SERVES 4

- 800g potatoes (around 700g once peeled)
- 40g butter or 2 tbsp coconut oil
- 1 onion (around 110g), peeled and finely diced
- 1 bay leaf
- 4 garlic cloves, peeled and crushed
- 1 tbsp ground or minced ginger
- 2 tsp ground turmeric
- 1 tsp ground cumin
- 1 tsp ground coriander
- Pinch of chilli powder
- 200g passata
- 150g frozen peas
- 1 tsp garam masala
- Salt
- Fresh coriander leaves, to serve

The onions and garlic in this recipe contain sulphur, which is required for the phase-2 detoxification pathway in the liver. So while this recipe won't 'detox' you, it does provide key nutrients your body needs to make detoxification enzymes. There are also a whole load of delicious spices here, but don't worry if you don't have them all, just try to include as many of them as possible.

Peel the potatoes and cut them into large cubes (around 3cm). Bring a medium deep saucepan of salted water to the boil and boil the potatoes for 10 minutes.

Melt half the butter or coconut oil in a large shallow saucepan over a medium heat. Add the onion and bay leaf and cook for 5 minutes. Add the garlic and ginger and cook for 5 minutes, stirring.

Drain the potatoes and add them back to the deep pan. Add the remaining butter or coconut oil along with a teaspoon of turmeric and return the pan to the heat. Fry for 5 minutes.

Add the rest of the spices (cumin, coriander, chilli and the rest of the turmeric) to the shallow pan with the onions and stir for 1 minute. Add the passata and the potatoes to the shallow pan, cover with a lid and gently cook for 10 minutes.

Stir in the frozen peas to thaw them and the garam masala. Season with salt and finish with fresh coriander.

BLACK DAHL

SERVES 3-4

- 250g black beluga lentils
- 25g butter or coconut oil
- 1 small onion (around 100g), peeled and finely diced
- 1 bay leaf
- 2 cardamom pods (don't worry if you don't have these)
- 2 garlic cloves
- 1 tbsp ground or minced ginger
- 1 tsp ground coriander
- 1 tsp ground cumin
- 1 tsp chilli powder
- 50g tomato purée
- 1 vegetable stock cube
- Salt
- 1-2 tsp garam masala
- 200ml double cream (or use oat cream)
- Butter, to serve (optional)

If you've ever been to Dishoom in London you'll understand the wonder that is black dahl. I don't have the time or inclination to cook something for 24 hours, so although my version isn't quite as good, I think it comes reasonably close. Onions and garlic are also a source of sulphur, which your liver needs for its detoxification enzymes.

Rinse the lentils until the water runs clear.

Melt the butter or coconut oil in a medium-sized saucepan and cook the diced onion for 5 minutes, along with the bay leaf and cardamom pods (if using).

Peel and crush the garlic and add to the pan along with the ginger. Cook for another 5 minutes.

Add the coriander, cumin and chilli powder and stir for a minute. Add the tomato purée and stir until thoroughly combined.

Add the stock cube, lentils and around 500ml of water. Bring to a gentle simmer, and cook for at least 30 minutes, ideally around 2 hours, adding more water regularly as needed.

Season well with salt and garam masala. Add the cream, and some extra butter if you feel like making it extra creamy! Stir until well combined and serve.

CABBAGE & CARROT CURRY

SERVES 3-4

- 2 carrots (around 240g)
- 250g white cabbage
- 2 tbsp coconut oil
- 1 tsp cumin seeds
- 1 tbsp ground ginger
- 1 tsp ground turmeric
- 1 tsp salt
- 1 fresh green chilli
- 1 tbsp desiccated or fresh coconut (optional)

This is the quickest curry recipe I've ever come up with. From start to finish, it takes about fifteen minutes, so it's great for when you're short on time. If you're one of those people who can handle curry on a hangover, this recipe is a great one, as cabbage is a member of the brassica family, and as such contains glucosinolates and other phytochemicals which encourage your liver's detoxification enzymes.

Dice the carrot finely (less than 1cm cubes) and finely slice the cabbage.

Heat the oil and cumin seeds in a wide-bottomed saucepan.

When the seeds are sizzling, add the rest of the spices and stir for 30 seconds.

Add the cabbage and carrot, and cook gently with the lid on for 5-7 minutes, until slightly tender but still crunchy.

Slice the chilli and stir in for another minute.

Add the coconut (if using) and serve.

CRUCIFEROUS TACOS WITH AVOCADO-YOGHURT DRESSING

MAKES 8 TACOS

- 2 tsp paprika
- 2 tsp ground cumin
- ½ tsp salt
- 1 tsp garlic powder or granules
- ½ tsp chilli powder or flakes (optional)
- 2 tbsp lime juice
- 3 tbsp olive oil
- 250g broccoli
- 250g cauliflower
- 1 x 400g tin of chickpeas, drained and rinsed
- 8 taco shells

For the dressing
- 1 medium avocado
- 200g natural yoghurt
- Juice of 1 lime
- Salt and pepper

Broccoli and cauliflower are both members of the brassica family, which contain phytochemicals such as glucosinolates. This chemical contains sulphur, which is required for the body's phase-2 detoxification pathways, and new research is currently underway to determine whether it has anti-cancer properties.

Preheat the oven to 200°C fan/220°C conventional/gas mark 6. Mix together the paprika, cumin, salt, garlic, chilli (if using), lime juice and olive oil to form a marinade.

Cut the broccoli and cauliflower into small florets. Spread over a baking tray with the chickpeas. Pour the marinade over the vegetables and toss to coat. Roast them in the oven for 30 minutes.

Meanwhile, make the avocado-yoghurt dressing. Place the avocado, yoghurt and lime juice in a food processor. (If you don't have one just mash with a fork until smooth.) Season with salt and pepper to taste. Place into a serving bowl.

Warm the taco shells for 30 seconds in a microwave. I'm a big fan of self-assembly when it comes to tacos, so I recommend placing everything in serving bowls in the middle of the table.

TIP Serve with chicken for extra protein.

GREENS & LEMON LINGUINE

SERVES 2

- 150g linguine
- 1 garlic clove, peeled
- 20g fresh basil
- 2 tbsp olive oil
- ½ lemon, zested and juiced
- Salt and pepper
- 200g fine asparagus, woody stems removed (or 150g tips)
- 80g frozen edamame beans
- 30g spinach leaves
- Grated Parmesan or vegetarian hard cheese, to serve
- Lemon wedges, to serve

This recipe uses crushed garlic, which helps release the phytochemical allicin, an organosulphate (so it contains sulphur), which has been linked to a range of health benefits. As it contains sulphur, it also provides a building block for the detoxification enzymes in the liver. Not to mention it taste delicious when mixed with basil and lemon!

Bring one large and one small pot of salted water to the boil. Cook the linguine in the large pot for 7 minutes.

In a food processor, blend together the garlic, basil, olive oil and lemon zest and juice, with a pinch of salt and pepper. Taste and add more seasoning if needed.

Cook the asparagus and edamame in the small pot for 3–5 minutes.

With 2 minutes left, add the spinach to the vegetables to wilt slightly. Drain most of the water from the linguine, and add the lemony sauce. Toss to coat.

Drain the vegetables. Divide the linguine and vegetables between two bowls, and add a sprinkling of Parmesan, along with an extra drizzle of oil and sprinkling of salt if needed. Serve with lemon wedges.

 TIP This would taste great with salmon added too.

MOROCCAN-STYLE BEAN STEW

SERVES 4

- Olive oil
- 1 onion (around 110g), peeled and finely diced
- 2 garlic cloves
- 1 tsp ground cinnamon
- 2 tsp ground cumin
- 2 tbsp ground coriander
- 2 tsp paprika
- ½ tsp chilli flakes
- 50g dates, stoned
- 200g carrots, cubed
- 250g sweet potato, peeled and cubed
- 1x 400g tin of chopped tomatoes
- 1 vegetable stock cube
- 1 orange or yellow pepper, chopped into 2cm cubes
- 1 x 400g tin of chickpeas, drained and rinsed
- 50g spinach leaves, chopped
- Salt and pepper
- Cooked rice, to serve
- Coriander leaves, to serve

It's all very well talking about the sulphur in onions and garlic and the way they help build the liver's detoxification enzymes, which they do, but enzymes are made of proteins and this recipe gives you all the amino acids your body needs by combining chickpeas with rice to form a complete protein source!

Heat a glug of oil in a large saucepan over a medium heat. Add the onion and cook for 5 minutes.

Peel and crush the garlic and add to the pan along with the spices. Stir for 1 minute. Add the dates, carrots and sweet potato and stir for 1 minute.

Add the chopped tomatoes along with a can full of water and the vegetable stock cube. Leave to simmer for 15–20 minutes, until the sweet potato and carrots are quite soft. If serving with rice, start cooking it at this point.

Add the chopped pepper and chickpeas to the pan and simmer for another 10 minutes.

Remove the pan from the heat and stir in the chopped spinach to wilt. Season to taste with salt and pepper.

Serve with rice and fresh coriander.

SPINACH & KALE DHAL

SERVES 4

- 400g red split lentils
- 1 tbsp coconut oil or ghee or vegetable oil
- 1 white onion (around 100g), peeled and diced
- 2 garlic cloves
- 1 tbsp ground ginger
- 1 tsp ground coriander
- ½ tsp chilli flakes
- 1 tbsp ground turmeric
- 1 tsp ground cumin
- ½ tsp ground cinnamon
- 1 vegetable stock cube
- 1 tomato (around 150g), diced
- 100g spinach leaves
- 50g roughly chopped kale
- Salt
- 1–2 tsp garam masala
- Fresh coriander leaves, to serve

I love dhal. I fell in love with it in India, of course, and have been obsessed with it ever since. I like using a combination of spinach and kale, because the spinach wilts until it's barely there, whereas the kale holds its shape a lot better, so the two complement each other nicely. Plus, there's the fact that kale is a member of the brassica family, and as much as it tastes vile raw, when cooked it's actually pretty decent.

Rinse the lentils until the water runs clear. Heat the oil or ghee in a medium saucepan over a medium heat.

Add the onion and reduce the heat to medium-low. Cook for 10 minutes. Peel and crush the garlic and add to the pan along with the ginger. Stir for a minute.

Add the rest of the spices (but not the garam masala) and stir for another minute. Dissolve the stock cube in 500ml of boiling water, then add to the pan along with the lentils.

Let it gently bubble away for 5 minutes, then add the diced tomato. After another 5 minutes, add the spinach and kale. Cook for another 5 minutes or so (around 15 minutes in total), until the lentils are cooked.

Turn off the heat and season with salt and garam masala. Taste and add more garam masala and salt if needed. Serve with fresh coriander.

MEDITERRANEAN STUFFED BUTTERNUT SQUASH

SERVES 4

- 1 butternut squash (around 1.2kg), halved and seeds removed
- Olive oil
- 100g quinoa (or 200g cooked grains)
- 1 lemon, halved
- 120g feta
- 80g sundried tomatoes
- 1 x 400g tin of chickpeas, drained and rinsed
- 30g spinach leaves
- Salt and pepper

Squash is a popular 'detox' food for some reason, along with lemons. I'm guessing the vitamin C probably has something to do with it, as vitamin C has an almost cult-like following. To be fair, vitamin C is important for liver function and repair, and as the body can't produce vitamin C, you do have to get it from your diet. If that means eating butternut squash occasionally I'm okay with that. I'd start with this recipe right here.

Preheat the oven to 200°C fan/220°C conventional/gas mark 7.

Drizzle the squash halves with olive oil and roast in the oven for around 30 minutes, until cooked through. Meanwhile, cook the quinoa in a pan of salted water as per the packet instructions, putting half a lemon into the pan, too.

Roughly chop the feta, sundried tomatoes and spinach leaves into chickpea-sized pieces. Drain and rinse the chickpeas. Add all of these to the cooked quinoa and stir well. Remove the lemon half from the cooked quinoa.

Season with salt and pepper and juice from the remaining half a lemon. Once the squash is ready, spoon the filling on top and serve.

TIP Scoop out some extra squash from each half to make room for more filling and save it for another salad or use it in place of sweet potato in another recipe.

SWEET POTATO MASALA DOSA

MAKES 6

- 100g gram flour
- 100g plain flour
- 200ml milk (any kind)
- Salt
- 750g sweet potatoes
- Vegetable oil
- 1 onion (around 100g), peeled and finely diced
- 4 garlic cloves
- 1 tbsp ground ginger or 4cm piece of fresh ginger, grated
- Small bunch of fresh coriander, leaves picked and stalks finely chopped
- 2 tsp ground turmeric
- 1 tsp ground coriander
- 1 tsp garam masala

Good old onions and garlic again. Have you noticed they've become a bit of a theme in this chapter? They are pretty damn amazing though, and the vitamin A-loaded sweet potatoes (an antioxidant) certainly won't do your liver any harm either. If you've never had a dosa before, you're in for a treat!

Preheat the oven to 200°C fan/220°C conventional/gas mark 7.

Mix together the flours, milk, a pinch of salt and 300ml of water and set aside. This will be your dosa batter.

Peel the sweet potato and chop into cubes, then drizzle with oil and salt and roast in the oven for 20–30 minutes, until nicely cooked through.

Heat a glug of vegetable oil in a large frying pan. Add the onion and peel and crush the garlic cloves into the pan. Fry for 5 minutes.

Add the ginger, chopped coriander stalks, turmeric and ground coriander and stir for another minute. Add 100ml of water and stir.

Once cooked, add the sweet potato to the pan and mash roughly, though not completely.

Add the garam masala and coriander leaves and season to taste. Transfer this filling to a bowl.>

SWEET POTATO MASALA DOSA cont.

Clean the pan and heat a small amount of oil, using a piece of kitchen towel to spread it around the pan.

Add a ladleful of the dosa batter so it just reaches the edges of the pan. Once it has almost cooked on top, place a large spoonful of the sweet potato filling in a line in the centre.

When the dosa is nice and brown and crisp underneath, use a spatula to gently fold one side of the dosa over the mixture and roll it in the pan (like wrapping a very hot fajita), so that the join is facing down into the pan. Cook for another minute before transferring to a plate.

Repeat this for each dosa, keeping them warm by placing the plate in a low oven between batches.

 TIP Serve with Indian chutneys and raita for those who like it less spicy.

ULTIMATE VEGGIE BRUNCH

SERVES 1

- 1 slice of sourdough bread
- Olive oil
- 80g tomatoes
- ½ large avocado
- Salt and pepper
- 3 slices of halloumi
- 1-2 medium eggs
- Coffee!

If you have a hangover and need to 'detox' your body of alcohol, this brunch should be top of your list of foods to eat. While there's nothing that can really speed up the process of metabolising alcohol except time, giving your body all the building blocks it needs to do that certainly helps. Here we have carbohydrates from the bread, fats from the avocado and halloumi, protein from the eggs and lycopene from the tomatoes. Lycopene is the phytochemical and antioxidant that makes tomatoes red and keeps your liver happy.

Get ready to multitask: place a large frying pan over a medium heat, bring a small saucepan of water to the boil and prepare your coffee.

Toast the bread.

Drizzle a little olive oil on one side of the frying pan.

Roughly chop the tomatoes and add them to that side.

Mash the avocado on the toast and season with salt and pepper.

Turn down the heat under the frying pan and add the halloumi to the other side of the pan. Cook for a few minutes on each side.

Crack the egg(s) into the boiling water and poach for 3 minutes, until the white is opaque.

Assemble everything on a plate and tuck in immediately.

Fats

THE 'FATS ARE BAD' MYTH

Many people will have had blood tests to check their cholesterol levels. Cholesterol is made by the body and regulated by the liver, but it can also be obtained from the diet. When you have your cholesterol levels checked, your results show the levels of low-density lipoprotein (LDL) (the "bad" cholesterol"), high-density lipoprotein (HDL) (the "good" cholesterol) and triglycerides (dietary fat) in your blood.

Overall, having high LDL, low HDL and high triglyceride levels produces the highest risk for heart disease. So how does this relate to our diet? Dietary fats have an effect on blood LDL levels, and therefore on the risk of heart disease. Trans fats have a negative effect and increase risk, whereas unsaturated fats have a beneficial effect and decrease risk. Saturated fat in itself isn't inherently bad for us, it depends on context. A diet that contains high amounts of saturated fat as a percentage of overall energy intake is linked to increased risk of heart disease. Evidence shows that reducing intake of saturated fat as a proportion of overall fat intake (but not reducing total fat) has beneficial effects, but replacing with unsaturated fats has a much more positive effect than replacing with sugar.

It's absolutely not necessary to eat low-fat. In fact, the Mediterranean diet, which is widely agreed to be a very healthy way of eating, is moderate-fat, and has a role for foods like cheese. This just goes to show that a whole-diet approach is more important. I like the message of moderation and the following recipes reflect that. I've used sources of saturated fat, especially cheese, as a bit of cheese is nothing to be afraid of.

PHYSICAL health should not come at the expense of MENTAL health

The same people who said we were stupid for believing a single nutrient (saturated fat) could cause all our problems are often now the same people blaming a single nutrient (sugar) for all our problems. Glad we all learnt our lesson there

ASPARAGUS & PEA TART

- 1 ready rolled puff pastry sheet (320g)
- 1 medium egg, beaten
- 250g ricotta
- ½ lemon, zested and juiced
- 1 tbsp olive oil, plus extra for drizzling
- 1 small garlic clove
- Sprig of fresh mint
- Sprig of fresh basil
- Salt and pepper
- 500g asparagus, woody ends removed
- 100g frozen peas
- 50g pea shoots

Ricotta isn't the most interesting of cheeses, but it tastes brilliant when paired with lemon, garlic and herbs. It contains saturated fats, yes, but that's not a reason you can't enjoy it in moderation, especially with such delicious vegetables!

Preheat the oven to 180°C fan/200°C conventional/gas mark 6. Line a flat surface with baking paper and unroll the pastry. Score a 2cm border around the edge and brush the surface with the beaten egg. Transfer the pastry on the baking paper to a baking tray and bake for around 15 minutes, until puffed up and golden.

Blend the ricotta, lemon juice and zest, oil, garlic, mint and basil in a blender or food processor until smooth. Season and adjust to taste.

Bring a medium saucepan of salted water to the boil. Add the asparagus and cook for 3 minutes (skip this stage if you have very fine asparagus or if you like very crunchy asparagus).

Place the cooked asparagus on a hot griddle pan. Drizzle with olive oil and cook on all sides. Add the peas to the asparagus water and cook for 3 minutes, or until they bob to the surface.

Remove the pastry from the oven and gently press down the middle rectangle, leaving the border puffed up.Spread the ricotta mixture evenly over the centre, then place the asparagus on top followed by the peas. Sprinkle with pea shoots before serving.

AUBERGINE HALLOUMI ROLLS

SERVES 2

- 1 aubergine (around 300g)
- Olive oil
- Salt and pepper
- 200g halloumi
- Small handful of fresh basil leaves, one per roll
- 50g salad leaves
- 100g tomatoes
- 1 tbsp rapeseed oil
- 1 tbsp balsamic vinegar

Halloumi is one of my favourite cheeses (doesn't everyone have a favourite cheese?), but it does go rubbery if you let it cool after cooking, so eat it quickly! As mentioned before, the saturated fat in cheese may be pretty neutral when it comes to heart disease, and context matters. By pairing it with ingredients such as aubergine, basil, oil and tomatoes, it's a great Mediterranean-style meal!

Preheat the oven to 200°C fan/220°C conventional/gas mark 7.

Slice the aubergine lengthways around 5mm thick. Heat a griddle pan and brush with olive oil. Grill the aubergine slices on both sides, seasoning with a little salt and pepper on each side. Set to one side to cool.

Slice the halloumi and cook on the griddle pan for a few minutes each side, then set aside.

Place a piece of halloumi on each aubergine slice with a basil leaf, then roll up roughly and place on a lined baking tray. Repeat this for each slice. Bake in the oven for 10 minutes.

In the meantime, make a salad with the leaves and tomatoes and any other items you desire, and divide it between two plates. Place a few of the aubergine halloumi rolls on each plate when ready to serve. Drizzle with rapeseed oil and balsamic vinegar.

BURRATA, PEA & MINT SALAD

- 1 slice of sourdough bread
- Olive oil
- Salt and pepper
- 100g frozen peas
- 50g pea shoots
- 1 tbsp fresh mint leaves, finely chopped
- Lemon juice
- 200g burrata (undrained weight)

Burrata is the king of cheeses. It's pure perfection and deserves to be the centrepiece of a dish. Combining it with greens gives this meal a perfect balance, and yes, that includes the saturated fat in the cheese.

Set the oven to grill or preheat to 200°C fan/220°C conventional/ gas mark 6.

Cut the sourdough into cubes, place on a lined baking tray and drizzle with olive oil, salt and pepper.

Grill for around 5–10 minutes or bake until the cubes are nicely crisped up like croutons.

In the meantime, bring a saucepan of water to the boil and cook the peas for 5 minutes.

Toss the pea shoots and mint together and drizzle with a little olive oil and lemon juice. Place the leaves on a large serving plate.

Once cooked, add the peas and croutons. Or leave them to cool first if you prefer.

Finally, carefully place the burrata on top, drizzle with olive oil and more lemon juice and season with salt and pepper.

FETA PARCELS WITH TZATZIKI

MAKES 12 PARCELS

- 200g spinach leaves
- 100g feta
- 2 spring onions, finely sliced
- 1 tsp dried or fresh oregano
- 1 tsp dried or fresh basil
- Salt and pepper
- 3 sheets of filo pastry
- Olive oil

For the tzatziki
- 80g cucumber
- 1 garlic clove
- 1 tbsp fresh or 1 tsp dried mint leaves
- 200g plain yoghurt
- 1 tbsp lemon juice

This chapter has essentially turned into an ode to cheese, which is perfectly fine by me. After all, pretty much all Mediterranean cultures eat cheese. These bite-sized parcels are quick, simple and delicious!

Preheat the oven to 200 fan/220°C conventional/gas mark 6.

Chop the spinach and wilt it slightly in a large saucepan with a little bit of water. Remove any excess water.

Crumble the feta into a bowl. Add the spring onions, wilted spinach, oregano and basil. Season with salt and pepper.

Cut a sheet of filo pastry in half, then in half again. You should have four strips, each of which needs to be folded in half to make four squares. Brush each pastry square with olive oil on both sides.

Place a heaped tablespoon of the feta mixture on the centre of each pastry square. Take the corners and scrunch up in the middle, then place on a lined baking tray. Repeat this for each of the four squares. Repeat steps 3–4 for the other two sheets.

Bake the parcels in the oven for 12 minutes. In the meantime, make the tzatziki: grate the cucumber, peel and crush the garlic and finely chop the mint. Mix together the yoghurt, cucumber, lemon juice, garlic and chopped mint. Season with salt and pepper.

When the filo parcels are ready, serve with the tzatziki.

FLAXSEED-CRUSTED TOFU BOWL

SERVES 1

- 100g firm tofu
- 2 tbsp lemon juice
- 2 tbsp light soy sauce
- 60g brown rice
- 10g fresh or dried breadcrumbs
- 10g ground flaxseed
- Sesame or olive oil
- 80g tenderstem broccoli
- ½ avocado, cubed
- Sesame seeds, toasted

Don't eat fish but want omega-3? Have some flaxseed. Add it to your smoothies, sprinkle it on your cereal or use it to elevate your tofu to the next level. No bland tofu here!

If the tofu isn't firm, press it by wrapping it up and placing something heavy on top for 10 minutes.

Cut the tofu into cubes, then place into a shallow bowl with 1 tablespoon of the lemon juice and 1 tablespoon of the soy sauce mixed together. Leave to marinate for 10 minutes.

Cook the brown rice in boiling water mixed with the remaining lemon juice and soy sauce according to the packet instructions.

Mix together the breadcrumbs and ground flaxseed in a bowl. Toss the tofu in the mixture until well coated.

Heat a glug of oil in a large frying pan and fry the tofu gently, turning occasionally to cook on all sides.

Steam the broccoli for 5 minutes or boil for 3 minutes.

To assemble the bowl, fill the bottom with warm brown rice, then place the broccoli, tofu and avocado on top. Drizzle over any remaining marinade and sprinkle with toasted sesame seeds.

LENTIL, FIG & AVOCADO SALAD WITH TAHINI DRESSING

SERVES 2

- 4 fresh figs
- 1 avocado
- 200g cooked puy lentils (100g raw)
- 50g rocket

For the dressing
- 2 tbsp tahini
- ¼ tsp salt
- ¼ tsp garlic granules or powder

Avocado is the ultimate 'healthy fats' champion. I don't think I've ever heard someone claim that avocados are bad for you, and that's saying something! Avocados are rich in unsaturated fats as well as containing vitamin E.

Cut the figs into quarters and the avocado into cubes.

Mix together the cooked lentils, figs, avocado and rocket in a serving bowl.

Mix together the tahini, salt and garlic granules or powder with 3 tablespoons of water.

Drizzle the dressing over the salad and serve.

MEXICAN FEAST

SERVES 4

- Olive oil
- 1 large onion (around 150g), peeled and sliced
- 1 orange pepper, sliced
- 1 yellow pepper, sliced
- 1 x 400g tin of black beans, drained and rinsed
- 1 x 400g tin of kidney beans, drained and rinsed
- 2 tbsp fajita spice mix (or make your own, see below)
- 250g cheddar cheese, grated
- 200g tomatoes
- 2 large avocados
- 50g salad leaves of choice, chopped
- Salt and pepper
- ½ lemon, juiced
- 8 tortillas

Whether you're into cheese or not, by cooking the beans and vegetables in this dish with olive oil, you're getting some heart-healthy monounsaturated fats with every mouthful!

Heat a glug of olive oil in a large frying pan over a medium heat. Add the onion and cook for 5 minutes before adding the peppers. Add about 50ml of water and let it simmer until the water has all gone.

Heat another glug of oil in a saucepan over a medium-low heat and add the beans. Stir for a minute, then add about 50ml of water and let it simmer until the water has all gone. Season the beans and the peppers with 1 tablespoon of fajita seasoning each. Add a little more water if needed to avoid things sticking to the bottom of the pan.

To make the salsa, season the tomato with salt, pepper and a little lemon juice. Set aside. To make the guacamole: mash the avocados in a bowl and season with salt, pepper and a little lemon juice. Set aside.

Put the salad leaves in a bowl. When the beans and peppers are ready, remove from the heat and pour into two serving dishes. Put the beans, peppers, tomato salsa, guacamole, cheese and salad on the table. Warm the tortillas in the microwave for 30 seconds and let everyone assemble their own perfect fajita.

TIP To make your own fajita seasoning, mix together 1 tsp onion powder, 1 tsp garlic granules or powder, 1 tsp paprika, 1 tsp cumin, 1 tsp salt and 1 tsp mild chilli powder.

MUSHROOMY MACARONI CHEESE

SERVES 2-3

- 150g dried pasta (macaroni or penne are best)
- 1 tbsp olive oil
- 2 heaped tbsp plain flour
- 350ml milk (any kind)
- 2 garlic cloves
- 200g white or brown mushrooms, sliced
- Salt and pepper
- 150g cheddar cheese, grated
- 20g Parmesan, grated

This recipe is dedicated to my sister Emily, whose love for macaroni cheese is slightly ironic considering too much dairy gives her digestive problems. Here we have cheddar and Parmesan cheese - a double whammy of deliciousness!

Cook the pasta in a large saucepan of salted water for 2 minutes less than packet instructions.

In a separate saucepan, heat the olive oil, then stir in the flour. Slowly whisk in the milk a little at a time, making sure any lumps are quickly removed.

Peel and crush the garlic and add to the sauce with the sliced mushrooms. Simmer gently over a low heat for 15 minutes.

Remove the pan from the heat and season the sauce with salt and pepper, then add most (but not all) of the cheddar. Stir until smooth.

Add the pasta to the sauce, mix together and pour into an ovenproof dish. Sprinkle the rest of the cheddar and all of the Parmesan on top.

Set the oven to grill and, when hot, grill the dish for about 5–10 minutes, until brown and crispy on top. Serve hot!

ASPARAGUS SALAD WITH CHICKPEAS & YOGHURT DRESSING

SERVES 2-3

- 1 courgette (around 200g)
- Olive oil
- Salt and pepper
- 250g asparagus
- 1 x 400g tin of chickpeas, drained and rinsed
- Paprika
- 50g salad leaves
- 10g pine nuts
- 150g Greek yoghurt
- 150g aubergine pesto (if you can't get hold of this, then follow the yoghurt dip from the roasted aubergine recipe on page 235)

Nuts are a great source of unsaturated fats, as well as fat-soluble vitamins like vitamin E. They make a great snack, but also taste great when sprinkled on salads like this one!

Cut the courgette lengthways into long, thin slices. Place in a microwaveable bowl, cover, and cook for 3 minutes on high.

Heat a little olive oil in a griddle pan on high heat, grill the courgette ribbons, sprinkling a little salt and pepper on both sides, and set aside.

Cook the asparagus by boiling or steaming for 5 minutes and set aside.

Put the chickpeas into a saucepan on medium heat with a little olive oil, salt and a pinch of paprika. Cook for around 5 minutes.

If you prefer, let the vegetables and chickpeas cool.

Assemble the salad: create a bed of salad leaves, add the asparagus and chickpeas, artfully (or not) place the courgette slices on top and sprinkle with pine nuts.

Mix the yoghurt and aubergine pesto together and dollop on top to serve.

TEX-MEX EGGS

- 250g sweet potato, peeled and cubed
- Olive oil
- 1 onion (around 80-100g), peeled and finely diced
- 1 tsp paprika
- 1 tsp ground cumin
- 1 x 400g tin of black beans, drained and rinsed
- 2 tbsp tomato purée
- Salt and pepper
- 1 lime
- 4 medium eggs
- 1 avocado, sliced

Eggs once had a bad rep, but now that we know the cholesterol in egg yolks isn't linked to increased risk of heart disease, you can enjoy this delicious meal without worrying about it!

Put the sweet potato cubes into a microwaveable bowl, cover, and microwave for 6–8 minutes on high, until soft.

Heat a glug of olive oil in a large frying pan over a medium heat and fry the diced onion for 5 minutes. Add the spices and beans to the pan along with a splash of water. Cook for 2 minutes.

Add the sweet potato and tomato purée and cook for another 2 minutes. Season with salt, pepper and lime juice.

Make four wells in the saucepan and crack in the eggs.

Add a lid if possible and cook over a low heat for around 8 minutes, until the egg whites are just cooked and the yolks are runny. If you're not a fan of runny eggs, then cook for around 12 minutes.

Place the avocado slices on top to serve.

Superfoods

THE SUPERFOOD MYTH

Despite the rise of the 'clean eating' movement that shuns processed foods and anything that isn't a 'whole food', we have also seen a rise in 'superfood' powders, which are definitely processed and not whole foods. Yet somehow we're led to believe that we need these for optimum health. These superfood powders include things like baobab, maca, spirulina, wheatgrass, and acai: you don't need them though, and here's why.

Baobab: If you're after vitamin C, there are so many easy ways to get vitamin C into your diet simply by eating certain fruits and vegetables like oranges, berries or peppers.

Maca: If you're after energy then coffee is your best friend. Coffee is not 'unhealthy', in fact it can actually reduce your risk of dying (as well as helping you not to kill people around you first thing in the morning). A lack of energy could also be a sign that you need more fuel (i.e. food) or that you're deficient in certain micronutrients such as B12 or iron. Maca won't treat the underlying issue there.

Spirulina: If plant sources of protein are what you're after, then I can recommend a whole host of alternatives that give you way more protein per serving and don't taste like pond water. Although they aren't always complete proteins, by combining them properly you can ensure every dish will have a complete set of essential amino acids.

Wheatgrass: If you're after more greens, then you're better off eating any green vegetable instead. I guarantee they'll taste better.

Acai: Supplementing with antioxidants may not be the best idea, but getting them from fruits and vegetables means you'll get a whole host of other benefits without the potentially risky high levels of vitamins.

So you see, you simply don't need them, as the following recipes will show.

The concept of 'real food' does not exist

The idea that you need expensive powders in order to be healthy is ridiculous and elitist. You can't negate an unhealthy lifestyle simply by consuming a teaspoon of green powder. It doesn't work that way. There's also nothing in these powders that you can't get easily and more cheaply elsewhere

ORANGE & BERRY SMOOTHIE

SERVES 1

- 1 banana (around 70-100g)
- 80g frozen blueberries
- 80g frozen strawberries
- 1 orange, juice and pulp
- 1 tbsp ground flaxseed

Sure, baobab can give you some vitamin C, but a single orange can give you your entire recommended daily intake, whilst tasting a whole lot better too. In this recipe, I recommend adding the orange pulp as well as the juice to get some extra fibre in there.

Put all the ingredients into a blender in the order written.

Blitz until smooth, scraping the sides of the blender if you need to.

Pour into a tall glass to serve.

SUMMER ROLL SALAD WITH MANGO DRESSING

SERVES 2

- 200g rice noodles
- 1 red pepper, finely sliced
- 100g cucumber, finely sliced
- 100g carrot, finely sliced
- 100g beansprouts
- Small handful of fresh mint leaves, roughly chopped
- Small handful of fresh Thai basil or coriander leaves, roughly chopped
- 1 red chilli, deseeded and finely sliced

For the dressing

- 1 mango (around 200g), peeled and chopped
- 1 lime, juiced
- Pinch of chilli flakes
- 1 tbsp soy sauce
- Small handful of fresh Thai basil or coriander leaves

I first made my own spring rolls on a boat in Ha Long Bay. They were the fried kind rather than the fresh kind, though. Unfortunately, rice paper isn't always easy to find, so I've decided to take the ingredients that would normally go in rice paper rolls and turn them into a salad instead. The dressing really makes it, and thanks to the mango, it also has plenty of vitamin C, more so than a serving of baobab anyway.

Cover the rice noodles in hot water and set aside.

To make the dressing, put the mango flesh into a blender or food processor with the lime juice, a pinch of chilli flakes, soy sauce and Thai basil or coriander and blend until smooth.

Drain the water off the noodles and mix in 2 tablespoons of the dressing.

Mix in the vegetables and the herbs.

Drizzle over the remaining dressing and sprinkle with fresh chilli.

TIP Want more protein? Try adding salmon, prawns, chicken or tofu to your salad.

MOCHA TRUFFLES

MAKES AROUND 20

- 200g dark chocolate
- 240ml double cream
- 2 tsp stevia
- 1 tbsp instant coffee
- Cocoa powder for dusting

Not only does coffee work wonders at waking you up in the morning, it also tastes great when mixed with chocolate and in desserts, which is more than can be said for maca. In my experience, everything maca touches ends up tasting like freeze-dried clay, and not at all like the caramel it's supposed to. Coffee, on the other hand, just makes everything better.

Break the chocolate into a bowl.

Heat the cream and stevia in a saucepan, until the edges begin to bubble.

Pour the cream onto the chocolate and stir until the chocolate has melted and the mixture is smooth and silky.

Add the instant coffee and taste. Add more if you feel like it.

Leave the mixture to cool in the fridge for 1–2 hours.

Once cooled, roll into small 10p-sized balls and coat in cocoa powder.

Chill for another hour in the fridge or until ready to serve.

COFFEE SMOOTHIE

SERVES 1

- 1 banana (100g if you like bitter coffee or 150g if you like it sweeter)
- 200ml milk of your choice (I like oat milk)
- 1 tsp instant coffee granules
- Pinch of cinnamon

If you need waking up in the morning, I promise you this will work way better than maca. Because that's what coffee is supposed to do.

Blend the ingredients together in a blender or food processor.

Taste. If too bitter, add more banana.

Serve.

VEGGIE PHO

SERVES 2

- Stir-fry oil or sesame oil
- 2 star anise
- 1 cinnamon stick
- ½ tsp whole cloves
- 1 white onion (around 110g), peeled and quartered
- 1 x 2.5cm piece of fresh ginger
- 1 vegetable stock cube
- Plenty of soy sauce
- 125g shiitake mushrooms, sliced
- 150g tofu, cubed
- 100g pak choy
- 200g rice noodles
- Bunch of fresh herbs: coriander, Thai basil, mint
- 1 spring onion, chopped
- 1 red chilli, deseeded and sliced (optional)

I was taught to make pho by an old Vietnamese lady in a one-to-one cooking class in Hoi An. This isn't that exact recipe, but it's pretty similar. Plus it contains tofu, which is a complete protein like spirulina, while tasting a thousand times better. Even if you don't like tofu, it still tastes better, because nothing tastes as terrible as pond.

Heat a glug of oil in a saucepan over a medium heat, then add the star anise, cinnamon stick and cloves and fry for 2 minutes. Add the onion quarters to the pan along with the fresh ginger, vegetable stock cube, 1 tablespoon of the soy sauce and 1 litre of water. This will form your stock. Cook this gently for 30 minutes.

In the meantime, fry the mushrooms in a little oil and soy sauce until soft. Remove from the pan and set aside.

Fry the tofu in a little oil and soy sauce. Remove from the pan and set aside. Cut the base off the pak choy and separate the leaves. Strain the stock and pour it back into the saucepan. Add the pak choy and leave for 5 minutes. Season well with extra soy sauce or salt.

Cook the noodles according to the packet instructions. Divide the noodles between two bowls and put the herbs, spring onions and chilli (if using) into serving bowls. Add the mushrooms and tofu to the broth and ladle it over the noodles. Sprinkle your bowl with a mixture of herbs, spring onions and chilli if you like it hot.

VEGETABLE & CHICKPEA PAELLA

SERVES 4

- Olive oil
- 1 onion (around 110g), peeled and finely diced
- 2 garlic cloves
- 1 vegetable stock cube
- 200g paella rice
- 1 tbsp paprika
- 1 tsp saffron
- 150g portabellini mushrooms, sliced
- 1 red pepper, sliced
- 1 yellow pepper, sliced
- 100g tomatoes, diced
- Salt and pepper
- 1 x 400g tin of chickpeas, drained and rinsed
- Chopped fresh parsley leaves, to serve

Spirulina may be a complete protein, but so is this meal. Combining rice and beans means this meal has all the amino acids your body needs. Seeing as a serving of spirulina has around 3g of protein, and this meal definitely has more, you're much better off just eating this. Also, it doesn't taste like a pond, so it automatically wins.

Heat a glug of olive oil in a deep-sided frying pan over a medium heat. Add the diced onion and stir for 5 minutes.

Peel and crush the garlic, add it to the pan and stir for another few minutes.

Pour 500ml of boiling water over the stock cube and stir until dissolved. Add the rice to the pan and stir for a few minutes, then add the vegetable stock.

Add the spices, followed by the veggies and season with salt and pepper. Add more water if and when needed to stop the rice from drying out. Stir regularly to avoid sticking.

When the rice is almost ready, add the chickpeas. Taste and adjust the seasoning if necessary, particularly if more salt is needed.

Serve immediately with a sprinkling of fresh parsley.

ASPARAGUS SOUP

SERVES 2

- Olive oil
- 3 garlic cloves
- 1 onion (around 110g), peeled and roughly chopped
- 500g asparagus
- 1 vegetable stock cube
- Salt and pepper
- 1-2 tbsp lemon juice

Asparagus tastes way better than wheatgrass. And asparagus soup tastes way better than wheatgrass soup. That's pretty much all you need to know!

Heat a glug of olive oil in a large saucepan over a medium heat.

Peel and crush the garlic and add it to the pan with the chopped onions. Fry for a couple of minutes.

Snap off the woody ends of the asparagus and cut the remaining part into thirds. Add these to the pan and stir for a couple of minutes.

Pour 700ml of boiling water over the stock cube and stir until completely dissolved. Add the stock to the pan and bring up to the boil.

Use a hand blender or food processor to transform the mixture into a deliciously creamy green soup. If the soup is not thick enough, return to the pan and allow it to cook down for a few more minutes over the heat.

Season with salt, pepper and lemon juice and serve with crusty bread.

GREENS & BEANS SALAD

SERVES 3-4

- 1 sweet potato (around 200g), peeled and cubed
- Olive oil
- Pinch of salt
- Pinch of paprika
- 250g asparagus
- 200g tenderstem broccoli
- 100g spinach leaves
- 1 large avocado, cubed
- 100g sugar snap peas
- 1 x 400g tin of chickpeas, drained and rinsed
- 1 x 400g tin of kidney beans, drained and rinsed
- 1 jar basil pesto (190g)

Wheatgrass tastes shit. Luckily green vegetables like broccoli, asparagus, sugar snap peas and spinach all taste great, especially all together. Conveniently, they all appear in this delicious salad that gives you six portions of vegetables (seven if you include the beans, and you should) all in one go.

Preheat the oven to 200°C fan/220°C conventional/gas mark 7.

Spread the sweet potato cubes over a baking tray, drizzle with olive oil and season with salt and paprika. Roast in the oven for around 20 minutes, until cooked through.

In the meantime, remove the woody ends from the asparagus and cut the stems into thirds.

Cut the broccoli in half. Steam or boil the broccoli for 5 minutes and the asparagus for 3-4 minutes, until slightly soft but still with some bite.

Slice large spinach leaves and cut the avocado into cubes.

Put everything into a bowl: cooked sweet potato, cooked greens, raw sugar snap peas, spinach, avocado, chickpeas and beans. Add the pesto and toss to coat.

BERRY CRUMBLE

SERVES 4-6

- 150g blueberries
- 150g strawberries
- 150g blackberries
- 2 tbsp maple syrup
- 175g plain white flour
- 125g unsalted butter, softened not melted
- 125g Demerara sugar
- 1 tsp cinnamon
- 2 tbsp rolled oats or flaked almonds
- Custard, vanilla sauce or yoghurt, to serve

Blueberries, strawberries and blackberries are wonderful examples of British berries. Why do you need acai berries from the other side of the world when we have perfectly good ones here? And they taste brilliant in crumbles.

Preheat the oven to 150°C fan/170°C conventional/gas mark 3.

Heat the berries and maple syrup in a saucepan and cook down gently for 15 minutes.

In a bowl, mix together the flour and butter with your hands to form a crumb.

Mix in the sugar, cinnamon and oats, again with your hands.

Pour the fruit into the bottom of a casserole dish.

Gently pour the crumble on top. Try to distribute it evenly and once it's on, don't spread it around.

Bake for 30 minutes, until the top is crunchy and delicious. Serve with custard, vanilla sauce, or yoghurt.

TIP You can also use frozen berries for this crumble – just defrost them before cooking and get rid of any excess water.

NO-ACAI BOWL

SERVES 1

- 1 frozen sliced banana (around 100-120g)
- 80g frozen blueberries
- 80g frozen strawberries
- Splash of milk (any works)
- Awesome toppings: banana slices, berries, coconut flakes, granola, sprigs of fresh mint

Acai bowls can be very hit-and-miss. I've had some really icy, horrible ones and some delicious ones, which also tended to have a load of other delicious ingredients in it like frozen blueberries. This makes sense, because the acai we get here doesn't really taste like much, whereas blueberries do. So why not save yourself some money (and air miles) by just making an acai bowl without the acai – a no-acai bowl.

You're going to need a strong blender for this one. Add the ingredients to the blender in the order shown.

Add the milk in small amounts, as needed. Be patient with it and scrape the sides of the blender often. The final mixture should be smooth and super thick.

Pour this into a bowl and assemble the toppings. Go haphazard if you're in a rush or place carefully to showcase it for Instagram. I won't judge.

Alkaline

THE ALKALINE MYTH

The alkaline diet is based on the premise that the body functions best in a slightly alkaline state, and that illness is due to acidity in the body. Proponents of the alkaline diet say that what we eat and drink affects the pH of our bodies, including of the blood. So we need to eat an abundance of alkaline-forming foods (mainly fruits and vegetables), and avoid acid-forming foods (meat, dairy and grains). This is a whole load of nutribollocks that goes beyond just simply eating more vegetables. Blood pH is so tightly controlled because anything more than a slight deviation either way is fatal. No food can compete with the army of enzymes and their pH demands, and no food will be able to alter the pH of your blood.

Health claims for the alkaline diet vary from the relatively benign weight management and reduced acne to cancer. Yes, they went there. They claim to be able to cure cancer. According to the leaders of this movement, cancer cannot survive in an alkaline environment, which is clearly bullshit, as if your blood were acidic you'd be dead.

Worrying about the pH of foods is completely unhelpful and unscientific. Many of the foods considered to be 'acidic' – such as most grains, beans, nuts, oils and cheese – have wonderful health benefits attached to them, not to mention they can transform the flavour of a dish and make it taste incredible. Hopefully, I've achieved that with this next set of recipes, and shown you that just because some of the ingredients are deemed to be 'acidic' doesn't mean you need to avoid them.

The alkaline diet plays on the fact that most people would have heard of pH and be vaguely familiar with it from GCSE chemistry, which immediately makes people think it's rooted in science, even though it's not

AUBERGINE PARMIGIANA

SERVES 2

- Olive oil
- 1 small onion (around 80-100g), peeled and roughly chopped
- 3 garlic cloves, peeled and crushed
- 1 x 400g tin of chopped tomatoes
- 1 tbsp tomato purée
- Salt and pepper
- Small bunch of fresh basil leaves, roughly chopped, plus extra for serving
- 1 aubergine (around 300g)
- 1 mozzarella ball (220g undrained weight)
- Finely grated Parmesan (as much as you want!)
- 20g fresh or dried breadcrumbs (optional)

This is a really delicious and impressive-looking veggie centrepiece. Sure, it has 'acidic' cheese but now you know that cheese doesn't actually leach calcium from your bones that shouldn't be a problem.

Preheat your oven to 180°C fan/200°C conventional/gas mark 6.

In a small saucepan, heat a little olive oil over a medium heat, then add the onion and fry for at least 5 minutes. Add the garlic and cook for another 5 minutes. Add the chopped tomatoes and the tomato purée. Allow to cook down for around 5 minutes, then season to taste with salt, pepper and a little basil. For a smooth sauce, blend to an even consistency. Or, if you prefer, you can leave it chunky.

Slice the aubergine almost all the way through but not quite so it's still all in one piece. Slice the mozzarella into thin slices. Pour the tomato sauce into the bottom of a large casserole dish

Place a piece of basil and a slice of mozzarella in between each aubergine segment. Put the aubergine on top of the tomato sauce. Sprinkle with a little Parmesan and the breadcrumbs (if using), and drizzle with olive oil. Cover with foil and place in the oven for 1 hour.

Remove the foil and add a generous amount of Parmesan. Put the dish back into the oven without the foil for another 10–15 minutes.

When ready, sprinkle a few more basil leaves on top and serve.

BLACK BEAN CHILLI

SERVES 3

- Olive or vegetable oil
- 1 onion (around 110g), peeled and finely diced
- 2 garlic cloves
- 1 tbsp paprika
- 1 tsp cumin
- Sprinkling of chilli flakes, to taste
- 1 x 400g tin of chopped tomatoes
- 1 vegetable stock cube
- 1 x 400g tin of black beans, drained and rinsed
- 1 x 400g tin of kidney beans, drained and rinsed
- Salt and pepper
- Plain yoghurt and fresh coriander, to serve

Did you know that beans are considered to be an 'acidic' food and therefore 'bad'? Doesn't make sense really considering they're such a wonderful source of protein and fibre. Ah well, at least they're combined here with nicely 'alkaline' onions and tomatoes, so I guess that balances it out? Oh wait, it doesn't matter, because the alkaline diet is bollocks. Phew.

Heat a little oil in a saucepan over a medium heat. Add the onion and cook for about 5 minutes.

Peel and crush the garlic and add to the onions. Stir for 2 minutes.

Add the paprika, cumin and chilli flakes. Stir for another minute.

Add the chopped tomatoes, then half fill the tin with water and add that too. Turn up the heat, and stir in the stock cube.

After 5 minutes, drain and rinse the beans, and add them to the pan.

Allow the chilli to cook down until much thicker, about 15–20 minutes.

Season with salt and pepper.

Serve with yoghurt and fresh coriander.

BUTTERNUT SQUASH LASAGNE

SERVES 6-8

- 1.4kg butternut squash
- Olive oil
- Salt and pepper
- 400g courgettes
- 1 onion (around 110g), peeled and finely diced
- 2 garlic cloves
- 680g passata
- 1 tbsp mixed herbs
- 1 tbsp chopped fresh basil
- 500ml crème fraîche
- 200g grated Parmesan
- 500g dried lasagne sheets
- 4 x 125g mozzarella balls, sliced

You will need
- A deep-sided ovenproof dish measuring approximately 23x33cm

Lasagne with vegetables instead of meat, surely that has to earn me some 'alkaline' points? Except for the fact that I've added a shitload of 'acidic' cheese, because, in my opinion, a lasagne without cheese just isn't worth having.

Preheat the oven to 200°C fan/220°C conventional/gas mark 7.

Peel the squash and slice into 5mm thick rings. Place on a lined baking tray, brush both sides with oil and season with salt and pepper. Roast in the oven for 30 minutes, then set aside to cool.

Thinly slice the courgettes lengthways, brush with olive oil and season with salt and pepper. Cook on both sides in a hot griddle pan or in the oven for a couple of minutes until cooked. Put to one side to cool.

To make the tomato sauce, heat a glug of olive oil in a small saucepan over a medium heat, add the diced onion and cook for 5 minutes.

Peel and crush the garlic and add to the pan, stirring for another 2 minutes.

Add the passata and herbs, and simmer for 15–20 minutes. >

BUTTERNUT SQUASH LASAGNE cont.

To make the white sauce, mix together the crème fraîche and 50g of the Parmesan, then season well with salt and pepper.

Lightly grease your dish with a little oil.

Time to layer up! Make sure to use quite thin layers of sauce so you have enough for all the layers. Start with a layer of lasagne sheets, followed by a thin layer of tomato sauce, some of the butternut squash, a thin layer of white sauce and a sprinkle of Parmesan, followed by more lasagne sheets, white sauce, courgette, more white sauce and more Parmesan and repeat the whole pattern. After the last lasagne sheets, finish with any of the remaining tomato sauce, a thick layer of mozzarella slices and the last of the Parmesan.

Turn the oven down to 170˚C fan/190˚C conventional/gas mark 5. Bake the lasagne for around 45 minutes, until golden brown and a knife slides through the lasagne sheets easily. Serve hot!

CHEESY MUFFINS

MAKES 9

- 200g wholemeal self-raising flour
- 100g courgette, grated and excess water removed
- 100g grated cheddar cheese, plus extra for sprinkling on top
- 100g cherry tomatoes, quartered
- 1 medium egg, beaten
- 50ml olive oil
- 150ml milk (any kind)
- 1 tsp paprika
- Salt and pepper

When something as basic as wheat flour is considered 'acidic' you know the alkaline diet really is a load of rubbish and just a disguised weight-loss diet. Eating these cheesy muffins won't make your body 'acidic'. Promise.

Preheat the oven to 200°C fan/220°C conventional/gas mark 7.

Mix all the ingredients together in a large bowl until fully incorporated and season with salt and pepper.

Fill nine muffin cases with equal amounts of the mixture.

Sprinkle some extra grated cheese on top of each one.

Place in the oven to bake for 15–20 minutes, until golden brown and an inserted toothpick comes out clean.

FALAFEL THREE WAYS

MAKES 8 FALAFEL

- Olive oil
- 1 small onion (around 80-100g), peeled and finely diced
- 1 x 400g tin of chickpeas, drained and rinsed
- 1 garlic clove
- 1 tbsp lemon juice
- 1 tbsp lemon zest
- 1 tsp ground cumin
- 1 tsp ground coriander
- 1 tsp mixed herbs
- 2 tbsp plain or wholemeal flour
- Salt and pepper

Variations
- Pink – add 150g cooked beetroot + 20g fresh breadcrumbs
- Green – add 10g fresh mint, parsley and basil
- Orange – add 200g cooked sweet potato, skin removed. Omit the flour

Not one, not two, but three kinds of falafel! So this is more like three recipes in one. Pick the one that sounds most appealing, or make all three and choose your favourite. Chickpeas are 'acidic'?! Oh come on, really? Screw this alkaline bollocks, and screw anyone who tells you that you can't eat falafel, you don't need that kind of negativity in your life.

Preheat the oven to 180°C fan/200°C conventional/gas mark 6.

Heat a little oil in a frying pan and cook the diced onions until soft.

Put the onions and into a food processor and add the remaining ingredients. Blitz until fully incorporated and smooth.

Form into 8 equal-sized balls and place on a baking tray lined with baking paper.

Place in the oven to bake for 15 minutes.

Remove the falafels from the oven and shallow fry in olive oil for a few minutes each side, until golden brown all over.

FULLY LOADED NACHOS

SERVES 4

- 200g salted tortilla chips
- 120g cheddar cheese, grated
- 1 x 400g tin of black beans, drained and rinsed
- 150g cherry tomatoes
- 2 tbsp lemon juice, plus wedges to serve
- Salt and pepper
- 1 large avocado (around 250g whole)
- Small handful of fresh coriander leaves (optional)

Corn is 'alkaline'! Rejoice and eat nachos to your heart's content. The acidic-yet-somehow-magically-alkaline lemon also makes an appearance.

Preheat the oven to 150°C fan/170°C conventional/gas mark 3.

In a shallow ovenproof dish or large plate, assemble a layer of tortilla chips with cheese and beans, then a second layer on top.

Bake in the oven until the cheese has melted.

In the meantime, make the salsa: finely dice the tomatoes and place in a small bowl with 1 tablespoon lemon juice and a pinch of salt.

To make the guacamole, mash the avocado in a small bowl with 1 tablespoon lemon juice and a pinch of salt and pepper.

When the cheese has melted, about 10 minutes, take the tortilla chips out of the oven, and dollop on the guacamole and salsa. Finish off with a sprinkling of fresh coriander leaves (if using) and serve with lemon wedges.

LENTIL & SWEET POTATO BURGERS

MAKES 4

- 100g red split lentils
- 150g sweet potato, peeled and chopped into 1-cm cubes
- 1 small onion (around 80g), peeled and very finely diced
- 1 garlic clove
- 1 tsp ground cumin
- 1 tsp paprika
- 1 tsp ground coriander
- Salt and pepper
- 10g fresh breadcrumbs
- 1 medium egg, beaten
- Olive oil
- Flour, for dusting
- Lettuce leaves, tomato slices, avocado and/or hummus, to serve

Combine 'acidic' lentils and 'alkaline' sweet potato and what do you get? A seriously delicious burger, that's what.

Cook the lentils in a pan of boiling salted water for 7 minutes then drain of all excess water.

Put the sweet potato in a mixing bowl and microwave for 5 minutes until soft. Mash roughly, then add the onion, garlic, lentils and spices. Season with salt and pepper then mix well and taste to check the seasoning. Mix in the breadcrumbs and egg.

Divide the mixture into four and form into burgers around 2–3cm thick. If the mixture is too dry to sork with, add a little oil. If it's too wet add a few more breadcrumbs or a little flour. Dusting your hands with flour can help with the shaping process, too.

Heat a frying pan over a medium heat, and add around 1 tablespoon of olive oil. When hot, place one burger gently in the frying pan and press down slightly with a spatula. Fry on both sides for a couple of minutes until slightly brown. Make sure to flip very carefully and no more than once to help them hold their shape. Add more olive oil each time you fry another burger. I recommend cooking them one at a time as they can be more delicate than meat-based burgers.

Serve in buns with lettuce, tomato, avocado and/or hummus.

RAINBOW VEGETABLE & HALLOUMI SKEWERS

MAKES 12

- 1 courgette (around 200g)
- 1 red pepper
- 1 yellow pepper
- 1 large red onion (around 150g)
- Olive oil
- Salt and pepper
- 200g halloumi
- sprigs of basil, to serve

You will need

- 12 skewers (if wooden, soak in water for 20 minutes before use to prevent burning)

All these rainbow vegetables on skewers won't do anything to your body's pH I'm afraid, no matter how 'alkaline' they apparently are. That doesn't mean you shouldn't eat them anyway, especially if you're having a barbecue in the sunshine.

Preheat the oven to 200°C fan/220°C conventional/gas mark 7.

Cut the courgette, peppers and onion into chunky cubes and spread them over a baking tray. Drizzle with olive oil, season with salt and pepper, and put them in the oven to roast for around 15 minutes.

Allow the vegetables to cool. In the meantime, cut the halloumi into cubes.

Assemble the skewers: a cube of red pepper, halloumi, yellow pepper, courgette, onion, and repeat once more. Repeat this for each skewer.

Heat a barbecue or griddle pan until very hot, and cook on each side for a few minutes.

Serve immediately with sprig of basil as part of a barbecue feast.

TIP Halloumi goes rubbery quickly when cooled, so only cook these just before you're ready to dish up!

RATATOUILLE QUICHE

SERVES 6-8

- 1 ready rolled shortcrust pastry sheet (320g)
- 1 aubergine (around 200g), sliced into 5mm-thick circles
- 1 green courgette (around 200g), sliced into 5mm-thick circles
- 1 yellow courgette (around 200g), sliced into 5mm-thick circles
- 100ml single cream
- 2 eggs, beaten
- 100g cheddar cheese, grated
- Small bunch of fresh basil, roughly chopped
- Salt and pepper
- 250g tomatoes
- Olive oil

You will need

- A loose-based tart tin approximately 25cm in diameter, greased with olive oil

This is the recipe you need if you're trying to impress. The key is to try to get vegetables with similar diameters, so think long, thin aubergines and wide courgettes. It's a wonderful balance of carbohydrates, fats, protein and includes plenty of vegetables. The cheese is considered 'acidic' so it's a good thing that doesn't matter!

Preheat the oven to 150°C fan/170°C conventional/gas mark 3.

Line the tart tin with pastry and blind bake for 15 minutes. In the meantime, microwave the aubergine and courgettes for 3 minutes.

Make the filling by mixing together the cream, egg, cheese and basil until well combined. Season and pour into the baked pastry case.

Assemble stacks of vegetable: an aubergine slice then tomato then yellow courgette then green. Take each of these and place them at a slight diagonal around the edge of the pastry to form a circle. Then repeat for an inner circle. You should have just enough to cover the whole quiche. Generously season with salt, pepper and olive oil.

Increase the oven temperature to 170°C fan/190°C conventional/gas mark 5.

Place a round piece of baking paper on top and bake for 30 minutes. Then take the paper off and bake for another 20 minutes. Leave to cool for 5 minutes before removing from the tin to serve.

SHAKSHUKA

SERVES 2

- Olive oil
- 1 garlic clove
- 1 red pepper, sliced
- 1 x 400g tin of chopped tomatoes
- Splash of water
- 1 tsp paprika
- ¼ – ½ tsp chilli flakes
- Salt and pepper
- 4 medium eggs
- Fresh coriander, to serve

In true alkaline diet nutribollocks fashion, eggs – a nutritional powerhouse – are on the naughty list. Don't listen to that; eggs are delicious, wonderful things, and are the star of the show in this brunch favourite.

Place a large frying pan over a medium heat and add a splash of olive oil.

Peel and crush the garlic and add it to the pan. Stir for 2 minutes.

Add the sliced peppers and cook for another few minutes. Don't char too much. Add the chopped tomatoes along with a splash of water.

Cook down for 5–10 minutes until a lot thicker. Then season with paprika, chilli flakes, salt and pepper. Taste and adjust the seasoning if necessary.

Make four little wells in the tomato sauce and break an egg into each one. Reduce the heat, and if you have a lid for your pan, place that on. For runny yolks, wait until the egg whites are just cooked, then take off the heat.

Serve with a sprinkling of fresh coriander (unless you hate it) and crusty bread.

Raw foods

THE RAW FOOD MYTH

Raw foodism centres around the incorrect belief that uncooked food is intrinsically healthier than cooked food. Firstly, there is no evidence to suggest humans were healthier when we only ate raw food. Experts believe that cooking likely contributed to human brain expansion, as it reduced the need for large teeth and jaw muscles, thereby allowing larger brain evolution.

On top of that, raw food does contain 'live' enzymes, yes. And cooking does denature these enzymes, thereby rendering them non-functional when heated above around 40°C. You know what else denatures enzymes? Your digestive system, duh. Your stomach sits at a comfortable pH of around 2–3 thanks to the production of gastric acids. That's highly acidic, as enzymes such as proteases which break down proteins function optimally in this kind of environment. Your body can't use plant enzymes; they get broken down in your stomach just like any other protein would, and your body uses the resulting amino acids as building blocks to make other proteins. Your body doesn't 'recruit' plant enzymes for its own use. Essentially, plants use plant enzymes, humans use human enzymes. End of.

Finally, cooking food may 'kill' (if you want to use such dramatic language) the enzymes in food, but that doesn't render the food 'toxic' or a nutritional wasteland. Cooking food kills bacteria and parasites that could harm you. In some cases, cooking food can break down some vitamins, yes, but in other cases it makes them more bioavailable (i.e. easier for your body to use).
So, it's not clear-cut and it really depends on the food.

In some cases, cooking food can break down some vitamins, but in other cases it makes them easier for your body to use

Some foods are more nutritious when cooked, others when raw, but these are not rules to live by, merely suggestions

ASIAN STIR-FRIED GREENS WITH TOFU

SERVES 2 AS A MAIN
OR 4 AS A SIDE

- 200g tenderstem broccoli (or regular broccoli if you prefer)
- 1 pak choy (around 100g)
- 1 tsp sesame seeds
- Sesame oil
- 2 garlic cloves, peeled and sliced
- 200g smoked tofu, diced
- 2 spring onions, sliced
- ½ fresh red chilli and a few Thai basil leaves (optional)

For the dressing
- 2 tbsp light soy sauce
- 1 tbsp sesame oil (or stir-fry oil)
- 1 tbsp grated ginger
- 1 tbsp lime juice
- 1 tbsp maple syrup, honey or rice syrup

Cooking greens like broccoli in water causes the vitamin C to leach out. By cooking them on very high heat for a short period of time instead, we can preserve more of the nutrients.

Chop the tenderstem broccoli into thirds (or if using regular, chop into bite-sized florets). Separate the pak choy leaves and slice any very big ones.

To make the dressing, mix together the soy sauce, sesame oil, ginger, lime juice and syrup.

Heat a wok over a medium heat and toast the sesame seeds for around 5 minutes. Set aside.

Turn up the heat and add a drizzle of oil.

Add the garlic and tofu and cook for around 5 minutes.

Add the rest of the vegetables along with around half the dressing. Cook for another 5 minutes.

Take off the heat and add the rest of the dressing. Sprinkle the toasted sesame seeds on top along with the chopped chilli and basil leaves (if using).

BEETROOT HUMMUS

SERVES 6-8

- 1 x 400g tin of chickpeas, drained and rinsed
- 250g cooked beetroot
- 1 garlic clove, peeled
- 2 tbsp tahini
- ½ lemon, juiced
- 100ml olive oil
- 2 tsp cumin
- Pinch of salt

Beetroots don't lose antioxidant activity when cooked, which is handy considering they're so much more palatable that way! Plus, it gives dishes like this one the most beautiful pink colour.

Put all the ingredients into a food processor in the order shown.

Blend until smooth.

Taste and adjust the seasoning as necessary.

 TIP This tastes great with my black bean burger on page 227!

BLACK BEAN BURGER

MAKES 3-4 BURGERS

- 1 x 400g tin of black beans, drained and rinsed
- 1 garlic clove
- 1 onion (around 110g), peeled and very finely diced
- 1 tsp paprika
- 1 tsp cumin
- ¼ tsp chilli powder
- 20g fresh or dried breadcrumbs
- Salt and pepper
- Olive oil
- Burger buns, beetroot hummus (page 224) and mixed slad leaves, to serve

When beans are cooked, both phytates and lectins are reduced, which means more nutrients for you and no toxicity either!

Pat the beans dry and put them into a large bowl. Peel and crush the garlic and add to the bowl along with the diced onion. Add the spices and breadcrumbs and season with salt and pepper.

Mash the mixture together slightly so it starts to coagulate, but leave at least half of the beans whole.

Heat a glug of olive oil in a frying pan over a medium heat.

Form a ball with a third to a quarter of the burger mixture, then gently press until slightly flat. For best results, the burger should be around 2–3cm thick. Bean burgers are more delicate than meat-based burgers, so make sure to form a tight ball of mixture, press it gently and fix any cracks. If the mixture is too crumbly, add an egg or a little oil; if it's too wet, cover your hands with a little flour before shaping the burger.

Fry this burger in the oil over a low heat for a couple of minutes on each side. Flip carefully and only once. Repeat with the remaining burger mix.

Serve in burger buns with beetroot hummus, avocado and mixed salad leaves.

CITRUS, RADISH & WATERCRESS SALAD

SERVES 1 OR 2 AS
A SIDE

- 1 orange (around 160g)
- 1 red or pink grapefruit (around 300g)
- 50g watercress
- 80g radishes, sliced
- ½ sliced avocado, or 30g crumbled feta, or 30g Boursin, or a combination

For the dressing
- 1 tsp wholegrain mustard
- 1 tbsp olive oil
- Pinch of sugar

The vitamin C in citrus fruits would be lost if cooked, so they are best eaten raw to get all the benefits! The cheese or avocado adds a creaminess that complements the sharp citrus nicely. You can add both if you like, I mainly wanted to include a vegan option here!

Segment the orange and grapefruit.

Place the watercress on a plate to create a bed of leaves and arrange the radishes and citrus segments on top.

Add the avocado or sprinkle over the cheese.

Mix together the mustard, olive oil and sugar to create the dressing and drizzle over the salad before serving.

GARLIC & ROSEMARY HASSELBACK POTATOES

SERVES 6-8 AS A SIDE

- 1kg Charlotte potatoes (these are the best ones for this but feel free to use other types)
- Olive oil
- 2 garlic cloves
- Salt and pepper
- 2 sprigs of fresh rosemary, finely chopped

Potatoes are definitely not meant to be eaten raw. But cooked they become things of beauty! Feel free to scale up or down as much as you like.

Preheat the oven to 220°C fan/240°C conventional/gas mark 9.

Put a potato on to a wooden spoon and cut very thin slices most of the way through the potato. The wooden spoon should stop you from slicing all the way through. Repeat until all the potatoes are finely sliced in this way.

Dip each potato into olive oil briefly and place on a baking tray.

Peel and crush the garlic over the top of the potatoes and sprinkle with salt, pepper and a little of the rosemary.

Roast in the oven for 30–40 minutes, depending on size, then add more fresh rosemary and roast for another 15 minutes.

Serve instead of roast potatoes with a roast dinner, or as a side along with a combination of salads, or any other way you like!

 TIP Serve this alongside a Sunday roast instead of standard roast potatoes.

PATATAS BRAVAS WITH ALLIOLI

SERVES 4-6 AS A SIDE

- 600g waxy potatoes, peeled and cut into 2-3cm chunks
- Olive oil
- Salt and pepper
- 1 small onion (around 80g), peeled and finely diced
- 1 x 400g tin of chopped tomatoes
- ½ tsp sugar
- ½ tsp salt
- 1 tsp paprika
- Chilli powder, to taste
- 1 tbsp sherry or wine vinegar (or use lemon juice)

For the allioli
- 1 egg yolk
- 4 garlic cloves
- 1 tbsp lemon juice
- 8 tbsp olive oil
- Salt

Poor potatoes have been demonised by the wellness industry as being 'empty calories', which is far from the truth. Potatoes contain nutrients such as vitamin B6, potassium, copper, vitamin C, manganese, phosphorus, niacin and fibre. But you won't get much out of them unless they're cooked!

Preheat the oven to 200°C fan/220°C conventional/gas mark 7.

Spread the potatoes over a baking tray and drizzle with olive oil. Toss to coat and season. Bake for 45 minutes, until crisp and golden.

To make the tomato sauce, heat a glug of olive oil in a saucepan over a medium heat. Add the onion and cook for around 5-8 minutes.

Add the chopped tomatoes, half a tin of water, sugar, salt, paprika and chilli powder. Stir and leave to gently simmer for around 20 minutes. When done, remove from the heat and stir in the vinegar.

To make the allioli, place the egg yolk, garlic and lemon juice in a food processor. Whizz until blended, then slowly drizzle in the olive oil over the course of a couple of minutes until it becomes thick and creamy. Season with salt.

I prefer to serve the potatoes and the sauces separately, or you can spoon the tomato sauce on top and serve the allioli on the side for those who can't handle the heat (like me)!

ROASTED AUBERGINE WITH YOGHURT & POMEGRANATE

SERVES 4

- 2 large aubergines (around 600g)
- Olive oil
- Salt and pepper
- 200g Greek yoghurt
- ½ lemon, juiced
- 2 tbsp finely chopped chives
- 50g pomegranate seeds
- Fresh coriander leaves, to serve

Raw aubergine contains the toxin solamine which can cause gut problems. But don't panic, you'd have to eat over thirty of them in one go for it to be a problem. Still, best to eat them cooked anyway, and luckily they taste better that way too.

Preheat the oven to 200°C fan/220°C conventional/gas mark 7.

Cut the aubergines in half lengthways and score the flesh in a criss-cross pattern. Place on a lined baking tray, drizzle with olive oil and season with salt and pepper.

Roast in the oven for around 15–20 minutes, until soft all the way through.

In the meantime, mix together the yoghurt, lemon juice, finely chopped chives and a pinch of salt and pepper.

When the aubergine halves are ready, spoon the yoghurt mixture on top and sprinkle with pomegranate seeds and fresh coriander.

TIP Why not serve with either the greens and beans salad on page 170 or the roasted tomato salad on page 236?

ROASTED TOMATO SALAD

SERVES 4 AS A SIDE

- Olive oil
- 400g small tomatoes (ideally a range of colours and sizes)
- 40g rocket
- 10g pine nuts
- Balsamic vinegar
- Salt and pepper

Tomatoes are most often eaten raw, but when cooked the lycopene is much more bioavailable, which means you get more nutrients from them!

Heat a griddle pan over a medium heat and drizzle with olive oil.

Halve the tomatoes lengthways. Place on the griddle pan flesh-side down, until gently seared.

Meanwhile, wash and dry the rocket and arrange on a serving plate. Place the cooked tomatoes on top, seared side up.

Sprinkle the pine nuts over the top.

Drizzle with balsamic vinegar and season with salt and pepper.

SPRING/SUMMER PIXIE PLATE

SERVES 1

- 80g carrots
- Olive oil
- Salt and pepper
- 80g asparagus
- Handful of salad leaves, such as spinach or rocket
- 60g red pepper, roughly chopped
- ½ avocado, cubed
- 80g cooked black beans

My Pixie Plates have become my signature style on Instagram. They contain a mix of raw and cooked vegetables, according to your liking. They're a great way to get a rainbow of delicious foods into your body!

Preheat the oven to 200°C fan/220°C conventional/gas mark 7.

Cut the carrots in halves or quarters, depending on size. Place on a baking tray, drizzle with olive oil and season with salt and pepper. Roast in the oven for 20 minutes.

Snap off the woody ends of the asparagus and boil in salted water for 5 minutes, steam for 5 minutes, or microwave on high for 3 minutes.

Assemble everything on a plate: salad leaves first, then arrange the rest of the ingredients on top. Season everything with salt and pepper and drizzle with a dressing of your choice.

AUTUMN/WINTER PIXIE PLATE

SERVES 1

- 100g butternut squash, peeled and diced
- 80g aubergine, sliced
- Olive oil
- Salt and pepper
- 40g puy lentils (80g cooked)
- 80g tenderstem broccoli
- 100g tomatoes
- Handful of salad leaves such as spinach or rocket

This plate is another perfect example of how using a mix of raw and cooked ingredients makes for a perfectly delicious balanced meal! Take the butternut squash, for example: the beta-carotene, lycopene and vitamin C in squash are all increased when roasted!

Preheat the oven to 200°C/220°C conventional/gas mark 6.

Spread the butternut squash and aubergine over a baking tray in a single layer, drizzle with olive oil and season with salt and pepper. Roast in the oven for 20 minutes, until soft.

If using raw lentils, cook these in boiling salted water (or with ¼ vegetable stock cube) for 20 minutes.

Cut the broccoli pieces in half. Boil in salted water for 4 minutes, steam for 5 minutes, or microwave on high for 2–3 minutes.

If using cherry tomatoes, cut each one in half. If using larger tomatoes, dice.

Assemble everything on a plate: salad leaves first, then arrange the rest of the ingredients on top.

Season the tomatoes with salt and pepper and add a dressing of your choice.

sugar

THE REFINED SUGAR MYTH

We have an epidemic of misunderstanding around sugar, with phrases such as 'sugar is toxic' and 'sugar is addictive' being spoken more often than they should be. Wellness bloggers will happily tell you that if you eat maple syrup or coconut sugar instead of white/caster sugar, you're eating a 'natural' and 'unprocessed' sugar rather than an 'unnatural' and 'processed' one. This is hugely misleading, as all sugars come from natural sources, and all are processed. You don't cut open a coconut palm and find coconut sugar pouring out in crystal form. Of course not.

The government guidelines, outlined in the SACN (Scientific Advisory Committee on Nutrition) report on carbohydrates in 2015, group all sugars into one category: free sugars. Which makes sense, because biochemically they're all almost exactly the same. The trace minerals found in sources like maple syrup are insignificant in the context of a healthy, balanced diet.

I think it's also important to point out that sugar is not addictive. Yes, it lights up the pleasure centres in your brain, but so does cuddling a puppy. That's not enough to determine addiction. Most of the evidence in this area comes from rat studies that do not mimic the conditions in which humans eat food. Humans don't generally experience long periods of total starvation followed by exposure to pure sugar, nor do we generally have to make a choice between sugar or cocaine.

If you're baking with sugar, then choose the type based on consistency and flavour, not nutrition, as they all count as free sugars and the nutritional differences are insignificant. That's exactly what I'm going to do in this next set of recipes. You'll find everything from golden syrup and maple syrup to caster.

Being SCARED of eating particular foods is not the basis for a healthy relationship with food

Categorising sugars into "refined" and "unrefined" is not only unhelpful, it's misleading and potentially damaging. All these sugars are processed, and all these sugars are natural

ALMOND BUTTER SWIRLED BROWNIES

MAKES 25 SMALL OR 16 LARGER BROWNIES

- 200g unsalted butter
- 200g dark chocolate
- 250g caster sugar
- 3 medium eggs, beaten
- ½ tsp vanilla bean paste
- Pinch of salt
- 100g plain flour
- 100g salted almond butter (or use unsalted almond butter and add salt)

You will need

- A 20x20cm brownie tin

The best brownies aren't made with sweet potato, cauliflower, aubergine or whatever fresh hell people come up with next. If you have a brownie craving, those things just won't satisfy you. What you really need are these. They have chocolate, sugar, gluten . . . the works.

Preheat the oven to 160°C /180°C conventional/ gas mark 3.

Melt the butter and chocolate together in the microwave or in a heatproof bowl over a saucepan of gently simmering water.

Stir in the sugar, eggs, vanilla bean paste and salt. Stir in the flour.

Line the brownie tin with baking paper and pour in the mixture.

Dollop over the almond butter and swirl the mixture together.

Bake in the oven for around 35 minutes, until just baked and super gooey.

Leave to cool for 15 minutes before cutting into squares.

TIP Not a fan of almond butter? Substitute your favourite nut butter or just leave it out entirely. Only have a loaf tin? Simply halve the mixture or bake in two batches.

BANANA BREAD

SERVES 8-12

- 300g plain flour
- 1 tsp baking powder
- 1 tsp bicarbonate of soda
- 1 tsp ground cinnamon
- Pinch of salt
- 2 eggs, beaten (use 6 tbsp aquafaba (chickpea water) to make it vegan)
- 100g maple syrup
- 6 tbsp olive oil
- 1 tsp vanilla bean paste or vanilla extract
- 50ml milk (oat milk works well too)
- 3 large, very ripe bananas (around 250-300g)
- Optional extras: 150g frozen berries or 150g chocolate chips
-

You will need
- A 1.5 litre loaf tin

For super moist banana bread, the combination of liquid sweeteners and spotty, ripe bananas is key. The extra flavour maple syrup gives over other sweeteners like rice syrup makes it my syrup of choice here. This is probably the sweet recipe with the lowest added sugar in the book! My favourite way to make this is with frozen blueberries, but other berries or chocolate chips work well too.

Preheat the oven to 180°C fan/200°C conventional/gas mark 6.

Mix together the dry ingredients in a bowl (flour, baking powder, bicarbonate of soda, cinnamon and salt).

Mix together the wet ingredients in a separate bowl (eggs, maple syrup, olive oil, vanilla bean paste or extract and milk).

Mash the bananas and add to the wet ingredients. Add the wet mixture to the dry.

Add the frozen berries or chocolate chips, if using.

Pour into a 1.5 litre loaf tin lined with baking paper or greased with a little oil. Bake in the oven for around 45 minutes, until an inserted toothpick comes out clean.

CHOCOLATE CHIP COOKIES

MAKES 10-12 LARGE
COOKIES OR 15
SMALLER ONES

- 6 tbsp olive oil
- 150g brown sugar
- 1 medium egg, beaten (use 4 tbsp aquafaba (chickpea water) to make it vegan)
- 1 tsp vanilla bean paste
- ½ tsp bicarbonate of soda
- Pinch of salt
- 200g plain flour
- 100g dark chocolate chips

I like my cookies slightly crunchy on the outside but soft and chewy on the inside. That's why this recipe uses brown sugar, as it helps provide the deliciously chewy texture that makes cookies so enticing!

Preheat the oven to 180°C fan/200°C conventional/gas mark 6.

Mix the oil, sugar, egg and vanilla bean paste together in a bowl.

Add the bicarbonate of soda and salt.

Slowly mix in the flour, a little at a time.

Stir in the chocolate chips.

Form 10-12 tablespoon-sized mounds or 15 smaller ones on a lined baking tray.

Bake in the oven for 12-15 minutes, until barely cooked and still soft to touch. If you've made 15 smaller cookies, bake for 12 minutes max, and if you've made 10-12 larger ones, test them at 12 minutes and bake for 15 minutes max.

Leave to cool for another 15 minutes before touching or moving them.

 TIP I actually prefer the texture of the vegan version of these, so give them a try!

CINNAMON ROLLS

- 240ml warm milk (any kind)
- 1 x 7g sachet of dried yeast
- 2 tbsp granulated sugar
- 1 tsp salt
- 45g butter, softened
- 1 large egg, beaten
- 380g plain flour (plus extra for dusting)

For the filling
- 100g butter
- 150g brown sugar, plus extra for sprinkling
- 2 tbsp ground cinnamon

These may take some time but they are oh so worth it. Sugar is vital to this recipe: it provides food for the yeast, which produces gases such as carbon dioxide in bubbles, causing the dough to rise. The soft brown sugar then melts perfectly into the butter and cinnamon in the filling, creating an overall deliciously doughy roll that you just can't get enough of.

Mix together the warm milk, yeast, sugar, salt, butter and egg. Make sure the milk isn't so hot that it kills the yeast! Mix in the flour and leave to one side to prove for an hour at room temperature.

Prepare the filling: melt the butter. Mix together the sugar and cinnamon. Line a large baking tray with baking paper.

Roll out the dough into a 30x45cm rectangle on a floured surface. Use as much flour as needed to ensure the dough doesn't stick. Brush generously with melted butter, all the way to the edges.

Sprinkle the cinnamon sugar on top, again spreading it all the way to the edges. Roll into a tight spiral, starting from the shorter end.

Slice into 12 pieces, placing each one cut-side down on the baking tray. Leave to prove for 30 minutes.

Preheat the oven to 160°C fan/180°C conventional/gas mark 4. Sprinkle with a little extra brown sugar and bake the rolls for 15–20 minutes, until golden brown on top.

FIG & ORANGE CAKE

- 200g unsalted butter (room temperature), plus extra for greasing the tins
- 200g golden caster sugar
- 1 orange, zested and juiced
- 4 medium eggs, beaten
- 200g self-raising flour
- 1 tsp baking powder

For the buttercream
- 75g unsalted butter (softened, not melted)
- 250g icing sugar
- 1 orange, zested and 1 tbsp juice

For the fig paste
- 1 fresh fig
- 1 tbsp runny honey

To decorate
- Orange and fig segments
- Rose petals
- Shelled pistachios (optional)

You will need
- Two 20cm diameter tins

Figs are my favourite fruit, but on their own I just don't think they provide enough flavour to a cake. Pair them with orange and there you have perfection! This cake combines an orange sponge with fig paste, orange buttercream and plenty of figs to decorate.

Preheat the oven to 160°C fan/180°C conventional/gas mark 4. Mix together the cake ingredients, adding the flour and baking powder last and folding in carefully.

Put half the cake mixture in each tin and bake for around 25 minutes, until golden and an inserted toothpick comes out clean. In the meantime, mix together the buttercream ingredients and chill.

For the fig paste, blitz the ingredients together in a food processor and store at room temperature.

Leave the cakes to cool before taking them out of their tins. If not serving immediately, refrigerate the sponges and assemble just before serving.

To assemble, choose the half with the least attractive top, and place it upside down on a serving plate. Add a thin layer of buttercream, then the fig paste, then another thin layer of buttercream. Carefully place the other cake half on top, right-side up. Gently add the rest of the buttercream on top and decorate with orange and fig segments, rose petals and pistachios (if using).

LEMON VANILLA CHEESECAKE

SERVES 8

- 250g digestive biscuits
- 100g butter, plus extra for greasing
- 500g cream cheese
- 100g icing sugar
- 1 tsp vanilla bean paste or essence
- 1 lemon, zested, and 1 tbsp of juice
- 200ml double cream
- Fresh fruit such as figs, blueberries, raspberries and cherries, and fresh mint, for topping

You will need
- A loose-based tart tin approximately 20cm in diameter

I've tried many a raw, dairy-free cheesecake in my wellness days, and while cashews do give a creamy texture, I find they're incredibly dense and have nothing on the real deal. This is the real deal, and it needs icing sugar because its incredibly fine texture allows it to be easily incorporated into a smooth, light mixture without the need for baking.

Grease the tart tin with a little butter and place a circle of baking paper in the bottom.

Crush the biscuits in a bowl. Melt the butter and mix into the biscuits. Press this into the base of the tin and leave to set in the fridge for 30–60 minutes.

Mix together the cream cheese, icing sugar, vanilla and lemon zest and juice. Lightly whip the double cream and fold this into the mixture.

Scoop this on top of the biscuit base and smooth out right to the edges. Put this back into the fridge for another few hours.

Just before serving, decorate with any fresh fruit you desire. I've used figs, blueberries, raspberries and cherries topped with sprigs of fresh mint.

TIP This can be kept in the fridge for up to a week.

RAINBOW FLAPJACKS

MAKES 8 SQUARES

50g soft unsalted butter, plus extra for greasing
200g rolled oats
150g golden syrup
1 tsp cinnamon
1 medium egg, beaten
Pinch of salt
50g blueberries (fresh or frozen)
50g cranberries
50g shelled pistachios

You will need
- A 1.5 litre loaf tin
- Double up the recipe to make a traybake

When I was younger, I was chief brownie-maker, while my sister was in charge of flapjacks. Now I make them both! Personally, I find your standard flapjack slightly too sweet, so I like to add berries and nuts, which provide a more interesting texture and cut through the sweetness a little. However, no flapjack is complete without a decent dose of golden syrup – it's what makes it so deliciously gooey!

Preheat the oven to 180°C fan/200°C conventional/gas mark 6.

If the butter is too hard, soften it with brief bursts in the microwave.

Cream the butter with the oats, syrup, cinnamon, egg and salt. Gently stir in the blueberries, cranberries and pistachios.

Grease the loaf tin with a little butter and line with baking paper. Pour the mixture into the tin and press down firmly. Bake for around 20 minutes, until golden brown.

Leave to cool for 5 minutes before removing from the tin and cutting into 8 pieces.

TIP These can be stored in an airtight container for up to 2 weeks.

PEAR & SALTED CARAMEL TART

SERVES 8-12

- 1 ready rolled shortcrust pastry sheet (320g)
- 50g granulated sugar
- 2 star anise
- 1 cinnamon stick
- 2 conference pears, peeled, halved and deseeded
- 375g caster sugar
- 100g golden syrup
- 100g butter
- 150ml double cream
- 1 tsp salt
- 50g chopped walnuts

You will need
- A loose-based tart tin approximately 25cm in diameter, greased

Proper caramel requires both a granulated and liquid sweetener. When they combine and work their magic you have the most delicious, thick, sweet mixture. Add the freshness of the pears and you have a winner.

Preheat the oven to 170°C fan/190°C conventional/gas mark 5.

Line the tart tin with the pastry, pressing gently into all corners and leaving some lightly overhanging. Prick the base with a fork and bake for 15 minutes. Leave to cool.

Bring 1 litre of water to the boil and add the granulated sugar, star anise and the cinnamon. Add the pears and poach for around 30 minutes, until a knife slides through easily. Remove and let cool.

Make the caramel: put 100ml of water into a pan along with the caster sugar and golden syrup. Simmer gently for 10–15 minutes, until the mixture is a deep brown caramel. Do not stir the mixture. Remove from the heat and add the butter, cream and salt. Stir until smooth, heating it slightly more if needed. Leave to cool slightly.

Once cool, place the pears on a board flat-side down and slice thinly.

Pour the caramel into the pastry case, fan out the pear slices, placing each fan gently on top of the caramel. Sprinkle the walnuts around the edges and in the centre. Chill for several hours, ideally overnight until set.

SUPER INDULGENT CHOCOLATE CAKE

SERVES 8

For the cake
- 150g butter
- 100g dark chocolate
- 1 tsp baking powder
- 30g cocoa powder
- 175g muscovado sugar
- 3 medium eggs, beaten
- 1 tsp vanilla bean paste or vanilla essence
- Pinch of salt
- 150g self-raising flour
- Chocolate shavings, to decorate

For the buttercream
- 150g dark chocolate
- 150g soft butter (not melted)
- 150g icing sugar

You will need
- Two 20cm springform cake tins, greased
- Electric mixer

No guilt-free bollocks here. This cake will satisfy all your chocolatey cravings and put a smile on your face. Don't waste your money buying raw cacao for this – you're going to bake it anyway! Muscovado sugar has a higher molasses content and has a slightly smoky aftertaste, which makes this chocolate cake taste even richer and more delicious.

Preheat the oven to 170°C fan/190°C conventional/gas mark 5.

Melt the butter and dark chocolate together in the microwave or in a heatproof bowl over a saucepan of gently simmering water. Add the rest of the cake ingredients and mix together, leaving the flour until last.

Divide the mixture evenly between the cake tins. Bake for 20–30 minutes, until an inserted toothpick comes out clean. Check every few minutes once it hits the 20-minute mark to avoid overbaking.

To make the buttercream, melt the dark chocolate in the microwave or in a heatproof bowl over a saucepan of gently simmering water. Use an electric mixer (if possible) to mix together the soft butter, melted chocolate and icing sugar until you have a thick buttercream.

When the cakes are ready, let cool completely. If you add the buttercream too soon it will split. Turn out the cakes, spread each with buttercream and place one on top of the other. Decorate with shaved chocolate and chill until 30 minutes before serving.

WHITE CHOCOLATE & RASPBERRY COOKIES

MAKES 10-12

- 7 tbsp olive oil
- 150g brown sugar
- 1 egg, beaten
- 1 tsp vanilla bean paste or vanilla essence
- Pinch of salt
- ½ tsp baking powder
- 180g plain flour
- 100g frozen raspberries
- 80-100g white chocolate chips

These cookies are dedicated to my sister Vivika, as it's her favourite flavour combination. I can definitely understand why. This recipe uses brown sugar as it helps provide the deliciously chewy texture.

Preheat the oven to 180°C fan/200°C conventional/gas mark 6.

In a bowl, mix together the olive oil, sugar, egg and vanilla bean paste or essence. Add the salt and baking powder and mix again. Add the flour, a little at a time, and mix until fully combined.

Chop the raspberries slightly - whole raspberries can make the cookies too soggy. Add the chocolate chips and raspberries to the cookie dough and stir.

Take tablespoons of the mixture and place them on a greased baking tray, spacing them out evenly. Gently form the dough into roughly round shapes. If any chocolate chips have come loose just press them on top.

Bake for 15-18 minutes, until the edges are just crispy but the middle is still soft.

Leave to cool for 15 minutes before touching or moving them.

INDEX

INDEX